IN GOD WE TRUST
EVERYTHING/EVERYDAY

Daily Devotional The BIBLE The King James Version

Always Trust God !

Shirley Nelson

SHIRLEY ROSE NELSON

WESTBOW
P R E S S®
A DIVISION OF THOMAS NELSON
& ZONDERVAN

WestBow Press books may be ordered through
booksellers or by contacting:

WestBow Press
A Division of Thomas Nelson & Zondervan
1663 Liberty Drive
Bloomington, IN 47403
www.westbowpress.com
844-714-3454

Scripture taken from the King James Version of the Bible.

ISBN: 978-1-6642-8383-1 (sc)
ISBN: 978-1-6642-8384-8 (hc)
ISBN: 978-1-6642-8382-4 (e)

Library of Congress Control Number: 2022921179

Print information available on the last page.

WestBow Press rev. date: 11/28/2022

IN GOD WE TRUST

The US motto, "In God We Trust," was first mentioned by Francis Scott Key in 1814 during the War of 1812.

According to the US Department of the Treasury, the motto, "In God We Trust," was first placed on United States coins in 1864, primarily due to the increased religious sentiment that existed during the Civil War.

During the height of the Cold War, President Dwight D. Eisenhower signed Public Law 140 on July 11, 1955, making it mandatory for all US coinage and paper currency to display the motto "In God We Trust."

In time of war, we turn to God. In time of tragedy, heartache, helplessness, and failures, we turn to God! He is our only source of hope and comfort, twenty-four hours a day, seven days a week.

He is the same yesterday, today, and tomorrow!

In God we trusted during the War of 1812, the Civil War, and the Cold War.

Give *me* that old-time religion!

JANUARY 1

It is better to trust the Lᴏʀᴅ than to put confidence in man. (Psalm 118:8)

We *all* face disappointment in our lives. We face different levels of disappoint at different times, from not getting a job, promotion, or loan; to not passing a test; to getting turned down for a date; to being told no; to not succeeding the first time or second or third time we try something; to not getting a good checkup from the doctor. There are many, many life disappointments.

JANUARY 2

He is not afraid of bad news; his heart is firm,
trusting in the Lord. (Psalm 112:7)

God, give me confidence in you!

Cancer is an ugly word. It takes you to your deepest fear.
The moment you hear that you, a family member, a coworker,
a teammate, or someone in the community has cancer, your
thoughts freeze, and fear and feelings of doom race in your
mind.

My uncles and one grandmother died of cancer caused by
smoking. One uncle died of melanoma.

In God we trust! Which cancer has struck your family
or friends? Did you turn to God? Can you handle the cancer
yourself? Not me! I have given many health problems to God.
Give them all to him! In God we trust!

JANUARY 3

When you pass through the waters, I will be with you; and when you pass through the rivers, they will not sweep over you. When you walk through the fire, you will not be burned/ the flames will not set you ablaze. (Isaiah 43:2)

Storms happen all over the world in everyone's environments. We have severe thunderstorms, flooding, ice storms, and tornadoes in our area. Nature's forces hit everyone, Christian and non-Christian alike. Have you had the fear of nature's forces in your life? In God we trust!

JANUARY 4

> But the fruit of the Spirit is love, joy, peace, patience, kindness, goodness, faithfulness. (Galatians 5:22)

Are you in pain? Are you dealing with health problems?

My body is slowly wearing out. My steps are slower, my eyes are weaker, my skin is thinner, and my thoughts are harder. My physical body is declining, but my inner spirit/soul is youthful and full of life. I like that! I have a soul that will never ever grow old. It will never die. It will live on and on, thanks to Jesus Christ, my Savior of my soul/spirit.

Find your spirit inside. Are you filled with God's Spirit?

If not, go to God in prayer. Don't wait!

JANUARY 5

Trust in the LORD with all your heart, and do not lean on your own understanding. In all your ways acknowledge him, and he will make straight your paths. (Proverbs 3:5–6)

I heard a sermon one time about worrying. The speaker said it was a *sin* to worry. That really got me thinking. Why worry if I truly believed in God?

In God we trust! Let God take *all* our worries!

It is also said that over 90 percent of the things we worry about *never* happen.

Give *all* your worries to God!

JANUARY 6

All scripture is breathed out of God and profitable for teaching for reproof for correction, and for training in righteousness. That the man of God may be complete, equipped for every good work. (2 Timothy 3:16–17)

Be prepared. I've tried to be prepared for everything. I've tried to prepare my kids and grandkids for what they might face. I like to overpack for ball games, bringing blankets, coats, chairs, snacks, raincoats, and sunscreen. You name it; I try to pack it! I want to be equipped. I want my family to be equipped.

But the best equipment in life is a Bible. Yes, a Bible. It covers every life situation for everyone—that means you and your situation!

JANUARY 7

Nevertheless he left not himself without witness,
in that he did good and gave us rain from heaven,
and fruitful seasons, filling our hearts with food
and gladness. (Acts 14:17)

Look around! God has provided so much. The crops are producing. We are able to raise potatoes, corn, beans, tomatoes, cucumbers, lettuce, cabbage, onions, squash, plums, and peaches. I love fresh strawberries and blueberries. The wild blackberries are ripening. Thank you, God! Fresh hay is being baled to provide food for the cows, horses, sheep, and goats for the winter. How amazing are God's wonderful gifts from each season! In God we trust!

JANUARY 8

If the Son there fore shall make you free ye shall
be free indeed. (John 8:36)

Fishing is not for me, unless they're biting every five minutes,
but my mom, husband, and grandsons would fish all day, every
day, in any weather. They just love to fish!

I wish I could be like Jesus and his disciples and be a fisher
of men. If people are not interested when I mention the power
of God and the love of Jesus, I need not be discouraged. God is
in charge of the outcome. I just need to keep throwing out the
lifeline.

If we would all fish for souls all day and every day, God
would provide the catch!

JANUARY 9

Come unto me, All ye that labour and are heavy laden, and I will give you rest, Take my yoke upon you, and learn of me: for I am meek and lowly in heart; and ye shall rest unto your souls. (Matthew 11: 28–29)

God has a strong message and a kind heart.

A man is getting a heart transplant today. He has been close to death for years with many ups and downs, and he has been on and off the long donor list. He has had numerous hospital stays. His family has had daily prayers, and he's been on church prayer lists. Today is the day he gets a young heart. Yes, the heart is from a young person, but the family doesn't know other details.

It's a sad day for the family who has lost the young, healthy family member—a sad, hard day.

May the young person leave the heart on earth to help others as his soul leaves to be with God in eternity. Jesus said, "Come to me." He left a message.

JANUARY 10

The blind receive their sight, and the lame walk, the lepers are cleansed and the deaf hear, the dead are raised up, and the poor have the gospel preached to them. And blessed is he, whosoever shall not be offended in me. (Matthew 11:5–6)

Jesus did amazing things while he was on earth.

Do you believe in Jesus? Do you have faith that he can do amazing things today on earth? Do you live your life believing in Jesus and his power to take care of you? Live a blessed life with Jesus!

JANUARY 11

Blessed is the man that trusteth in the Lord, and whose hope the Lord is, For he shall be as a tree planted by the waters, and spreadeth out her roots by the river, and shall not see when heat cometh but her leaf shall be green: and shall not be careful in the year of drought, neither shall cease from yielding fruit. (Jeremiah 17:7–8)

God reminds us to trust in him. We all go through periods of drought in our physical lives, our emotional lives, and our spiritual lives. Things dry up, and everything turns brown and lifeless. But God is our source of new and everlasting life. Thank you, God!

JANUARY 12

Cause me to hear thy loving: kindness in the morning: for in *thee do I trust*: cause me to know the way where in I should walk; for I lift up my soul unto thee. (Psalm 143:8, emphasis added)

Good morning, Lord. Let me be thankful for the day and life before me this day and every day! Let me end my day with a "thank you, Lord" for the blessings and the trust I have in you, God. Lift up my soul daily to withstand the trials I face.

JANUARY 13

He that handleth a matter wisely shall find good;
and whoso trusteth in the Lord, happy is he.
(Proverbs 16:20)

The Bible has many verses about being wise. It always feels
better to be wise than to be a fool. God reminds us to be wise,
to choose wisely, and to trust him. Can't go wrong with that
advice. Happy is he, you, and me!

JANUARY 14

What time I am afraid, I will Trust in Thee.
(Psalm 56:3)

Everyone gets afraid of something, sometime—everyone! We fear the unknown, the future, failure, life without answers, or the deaths of ourselves or others. We all have been afraid, but God is there. Trust in him.

JANUARY 15

And whatsoever we ask, we receive of him, because we *keep* his commandments, and do those things that are pleasing in his sight. (1 John 3:22, emphasis added)

The key word in today's verse is *keep*. Do you keep God's commandments? *All* of them? What do you do daily? Is it pleasing in his sight? No one knows your heart and life but you and God. God sees your actions, thoughts, and heart. He always listens to your requests. Keep his commandments. Ask for whatever you need, not whatever you want. In God we trust.

JANUARY 16

Commit thy way unto the Lord: trust also in him:
and he shall bring it to pass. (Psalm 37:5)

Commit means to pledge or bind. Fully dedicate yourself to something. God wants you to listen fully and to obey him. God wants you to *trust* him. He will fulfill his promises, and eternity is coming!

JANUARY 17

But I trusted in thee, O Lord: I said, Thou art my God. My times are in they hand: deliver me from the hand of mine enemies, and from them that persecute Me. (Psalm 31:14–15)

"I can't handle it anymore, God!" Have you ever had that feeling? Everyone has felt helpless. You might have felt that you were fighting a battle alone. Stand strong, and stand tough. God is with you. Pray and wait! In God we trust.

JANUARY 18

In thee, O Lord, do I put my trust: let me never
be ashamed: deliver me in they righteousness.
(Psalm 31:1)

Pray the following prayer: "God help me." Pray for God to hear
your sincere requests. Pray for patience to wait on the Lord.
Pray, and trust in God. He answers prayers for your best in his
own time, not yours.

JANUARY 19

Thou shalt have no other gods before me.
(Exodus 20:3)

What do you put before God? What's more important to you than God? These are questions that only you can answer.

Each day when your feet hit the floor, thank God for a new day to honor and live for him.

Put God first, and everything else will be taken care of in a way that *only* God can do.

JANUARY 20

And the Lord God formed man of the dust of the ground and breathed into his nostrils the breath of life: and man became a "Living Soul." (Genesis 2:7)

You were made by God. He has special plans for just you! He wants to help, guide, forgive, love, and prepare you for eternity.

Everyone will die, but where will your soul spend eternity?

You have to make that choice and live with it. Decide to accept Jesus as God's Son, who died to save your soul.

Heaven or hell? Live life for your Creator!

JANUARY 21

Esau ran to meet him [his estranged brother, Jacob] and embraced him, and fell on his neck, and kissed him: and they wept. (Genesis 33:4)

Lord, you know the burden, hurt, and pain that my brother has inflicted upon my family and my life, yet you still forgive.

Please give me the eyes and heart to be like you. In God I trust!

Do you have a family member, friend, neighbor, coworker, church member, or classmate who has given you pain, disappointment, or grief?

God's love is greater than all the burdens these people have brought to you.

I want to live with the heart of love and forgiveness.

Thank you, Lord.

JANUARY 22

Jesus said, "Let the little children come to me, and do not stop them: for it is to such as these that the Kingdom of Heaven belongs." (Matthew 19:14)

Children are God's most treasured blessings. Their laughter fills the soul with joy. We must remember we are all God's children. Look into people's souls, not the outward appearance. What does God see in you and others?

JANUARY 23

He is not afraid of bad news: his heart is firm,
trusting in the Lord. (Psalm 112:7)

Yes, I'm afraid of bad news, but my heart is firm in trusting God.
My first human reaction is to panic, to think, *Woe is me and the
situation I'm facing.*

I have to fight the devil's thoughts that he puts in my mind.
I say, "Flee from me, Satan! The Lord, my God, is in charge! He
is the almighty, and I trust God with any and all my situations!"

In God I trust!

JANUARY 24

Many are the sorrows of the wicked, but steadfast love surrounds the one who trusts in the Lord. (Psalm 32:10)

Facing the reality of death can be a hopeless defeat or a rejoicing comfort and peace. The difference is in the belief and trust in God. You can't give anyone hope, peace, or comfort if they don't know Jesus as their personal Savior.

Hope, peace, comfort, and heaven come only from believing and trusting God.

Do you believe and trust?

JANUARY 25

Wait for the Lord: be strong and take heart and
wait for the Lord. (Psalm 27: 14)

God is the *only* reason I've made it this far.

I thought growing old would take longer, but my hands
show my age!

Ask not what God can do for you but what you can do this
day—and the days ahead—for God.

JANUARY 26

Commit to the Lord whatever you do, and he
will establish your plans. (Proverbs 16:3)

A new year, a new beginning; a new mind, body, soul, and
spirit.

Turn your entire life to God.

Go into each new day, praying for wisdom, and commit
everything you do in honor to God.

In God we trust everything for the new day and new year.

JANUARY 27

God is our Refuge and strength, an ever-present
help in trouble. (Psalm 46: 1)

Everything seems to be falling apart. Nothing seems to be working. All my problems have compounded. I can't see how I can keep going or survive today, this week, this month, or this year. God is in the room, car, house, school, game, office, situation, and any environment.

In God we trust, now and forever!

Repeat the following: God is *my* refuge and strength, an ever-present help in trouble!

JANUARY 28

Thou, which hast shewed me great and sore troubles, Shalt quicken me again, and shalt bring me up again from the depths of the earth. Thou shalt increase my greatness, and comfort me on every side. (Psalm 71:20–21)

Everyone—old, young, rich, poor, educated, uneducated—has suffered from hardships. God will restore you. God changes despair, failure, depression, broken dreams, and disasters of all kinds.

Over and over again in my life—and in your life too—God has restored me and you.

God has allowed comebacks in my life, better than I could ever have dreamed or imagined.

JANUARY 29

Blessed are they that mourn: for they shall be
comforted. (Matthew 5:4)

Everyone will die. Everyone will grieve. I have seen babies,
kids, teenagers, young adults, mothers, fathers, sisters,
brothers, sons, daughters, grandparents, aunts, uncles, cousins,
roommates, neighbors, friends, coworkers, athletes, coaches,
teachers, government officials, students, the unborn, and those
over 100 years old die.

Everyone will die. Everyone will grieve.

Only God can give true comfort—*if* those who die are in
heaven.

Will your loved ones on earth feel peace and comfort when
you die? Will you be in heaven or hell?

JANUARY 30

Now our Lord Jesus Christ himself, and God,
even our Father, which hath loved us, and hath
given us everlasting consolation and good hope
through grace. (2 Thessalonians 2:16)

Two close friends, two sons—one friend and her son were
Christians. The other friend and her son were nonbelievers.

Both sons died tragically in their twenties.

One friend had the comfort of the eternal peace of God,
knowing she would see her Christian son again in heaven—
God's eternal promise!

The other friend did not have any comfort or peace. She
died a few years later, brokenhearted.

Do you have God in your life and in death?

JANUARY 31

But they that wait upon the LORD shall renew their strength: they shall mount up with wings as eagles: they shall run and not faint. (Isaiah 40:31)

Depression is a word we hear over and over, daily, from youth, adults, and seniors.

Medications and counseling help patch the problem of depression. Drugs and alcohol also only patch the problem.

These do not cure depression.

Only God can cure, reverse, or turn around your depression. Turn to God for a renewal of your spirit. Get personal treatment from God, twenty-four/seven.

FEBRUARY 1

The Lᴏʀᴅ thy God in the midst of thee is mighty:
he will save, he will rejoice over thee with joy:
he will rest in his love, he will joy over thee with
singing. (Zephaniah 3:17)

Don't feel hopeless, alone, or despairing. God is with you.

Look for the little and big blessings in your life, past and present. God was and is there with each blessing. God has plans just for you.

I love the following saying—think about it:

Anyone can count the seeds in one apple but only God can count the apples in one seed.

He knows you can grow and have many new blessings.

In God we trust.

FEBRUARY 2

And he said, The LORD is my rock, and my fortress, and my deliverer; The God of my rock; in him will I trust; he is my shield, and the horn of my salvation my high tower, and my refuge, me savior; thou savest me from violence. (2 Samuel 22:2–3)

Read the verse again, and place emphasis on the word *my.*

It's personal! God is personal, just for you. Don't feel defeated or alone. He is *your* Savior, twenty-four/seven.

In God we trust.

FEBRUARY 3

For thou art my hope, O Lord God; thou art my
trust from my youth. (Psalm 71:5)

I was blessed in my youth with Christian adults and a Christian
environment. I got to see God at work in my youth, and those
experiences only grew from year to year into my adult life.

Your hope and trust can begin at any age. God is available
and visible, twenty-four/seven!

Are you looking?

My hope, my trust is with God.

FEBRUARY 4

Be careful for nothing; but in *every* thing by
prayer and supplication with thanksgiving
let your requests be made know unto God.
(Philippians 4:6, emphasis added)

When a problem arises or things go wrong, it's human nature
to try to fix it ourselves. When the issue is overwhelming or
too big for us, that's when we turn to God. The above verse is
a constant reminder to turn to God *first* in everything, big or
small. Go to God daily, first thing in the morning, and give your
prayers and requests to God. Start each day with a personal,
trusting relationship with God.

FEBRUARY 5

Therefore I will look unto the Lord; I will wait
for the God of my salvation; my God will hear
me. (Micah 7:7)

Turn your thoughts and prayers to God. He is listening and does
hear you. He will do what is best for you. It's hard to wait for
anything but extra hard when you're waiting for God's answer,
and you want it *now*.

God does hear you. Keep calm and pray.

In God we trust

FEBRUARY 6

And the peace of God, which passeth all understanding, shall keep your hearts and minds through Christ Jesus. (Philippians 4:7)

Peace—true peace—can only be found in God and the Holy Spirit who lives inside you, *if* you have received it through Jesus Christ.

Do you have peace? If not, seek it. God is with you. Search daily to be a part of God's love.

FEBRUARY 7

> But without faith it is impossible to please him;
> for he that cometh to God must believe that
> he is, and that he is a rewarder of them that
> *diligently* seek him. (Hebrews 11:6, emphasis
> added)

A soul without God is lost. It is without peace or comfort, a life on earth without a spirit life after death.

It is up to you. God loves you.

Seek him! Open your eyes and see the world that God has made. Feel the air you breathe in your lungs. Touch the beauty of life. *That* is God.

I am *nothing* without God.

FEBRUARY 8

Now the God of hope fill you with all joy and peace in believing, that ye may abound in hope, through the power of the Holy Ghost. (Romans 15:13)

When you accept God, totally accept him and believe in his Son, Jesus Christ.

You are filled with the Holy Ghost. Now you will abound with hope.

There is nothing stronger or bigger than God!

FEBRUARY 9

But God commendeth his love toward us, in that
while we were yet sinners, Christ died for us.
(Romans 5:8)

There it is again: Jesus Christ died for us (you)! He showed
an unconditional love that carries us (you) to eternity to be
with him.

In God we trust!

FEBRUARY 10

Jesus said:

> Let not your heart be troubled ye believe in God believe also in me. In my Father's house are many mansions: if it were not so I would have told you. And if I go and prepare a place for you, I will come again and receive you unto myself; that where I am, there ye may be also. (John 14: 1–3)

Thank you for your promise, Jesus!

FEBRUARY 11

And if we know that he "hear" us, whatsoever we ask, we *know* that we have the petitions that we desired of him. (1 John 5:15, emphasis added)

God is with us. He hears and listens! Pray often each day, multiple times.

Pray prayers of thanksgiving.

Pray for others.

Pray for your needs, *not* your wants.

Pray for a pure heart and a good spirit to let your light shine.

FEBRUARY 12

It is better to trust in the Lord than to put confidence in man. (Psalm 118:8)

Individuals come with their own problems. People will let you down. You cannot put confidence in men or women.

God cares for you. God provides hope, comfort, and peace. God promises an eternal spiritual home.

Put your trust in God.

FEBRUARY 13

Jesus said:

> Let not your heart be troubled: ye believe in God
> believe also in me. (John 14:1)

Jesus knows you are human. You will have trials, pain, problems, drama, sickness, heartache, depression, stress, and many troubling times.

Jesus also knows that God is with you.

Believe and trust God. Jesus died for you. Give your troubles to God.

FEBRUARY 14

Thou wilt keep him in perfect peace, whose
mind is stayed on thee; because he trusteth in
thee. (Isaiah 26:3)

God provides the "perfect peace."

Your mind, body, and soul can find the perfect peace if you
seek to be completely with God's love and promises. You have
to have that loving, trusting relationship with God.

Seek his promises in the Bible. Keep your mind and heart
with God.

God's precious promises can be found in the following
verses:

James 1:5
Psalm 37:4
Philippians 4:4–7
Psalm 103:1–3
Romans 8:38–39
John 14:1–3

FEBRUARY 15

The Lord is my strength and my shield; my
heart trusted in him and I am helped; therefore
my heart greatly rejoiceth; with my song will I
praise him. (Psalm 28:7)

Thank you, Lord, for being my strength when I am weak. Thank
you, Lord, for being my shield against the things, people, and
problems from which I cannot defend myself.

My heart greatly rejoiceth (rejoices) that God is great inside
my soul.

FEBRUARY 16

What time I am afraid, I will trust in thee. In
God I will praise his word, in God I have put my
trust' I will not fear what flesh can do unto me.
(Psalm 56:3–4)

Everyone will die. All flesh will fail us. Our bodies will stop
working.

Just like Jesus, we will experience physical, bodily death.

Like Jesus, when we believe the death is defeated and that
our peace comes from the Spirit, we will live again in a heavenly
Spirit for eternity.

In God we trust!

FEBRUARY 17

Jesus said:

> Even the Spirit of truth; whom the world cannot
> receive, because it seeth him not, neither
> knoweth him; but ye know him; for he dwelleth
> with you, and shall be *in you.* (John 14:17,
> emphasis added)

When Jesus becomes real to you and you believe and accept
him into your life, the Holy Spirit becomes an unseen part of
you. The unseen can be felt within you. You realize that you are
more than an earthly body.

In God the Father, the Son, and the Holy Ghost ... we *trust!*

FEBRUARY 18

Commit thy way unto the Lord; trust also in
him; and he shall bring it to pass. (Psalm 37:5)

To conflicting forces, good and evil cannot exist in one heart.
Where evil is present, good cannot dwell.

Give your heart totally to God. Ensure that there is *no* place
for evil to dwell.

Trust in God, every second of every day.

FEBRUARY 19

Not that I speak in respect of want; for I have learned, in whatever state I am there with to be content. (Philippians 4: 11)

It's hard to be content during these times of trying to achieve more and more. People want bigger houses, more power, more money, fancier cars, showier possessions, and a bigger and more abundant lifestyle.

You cannot take even one of these things with you after death. Jesus is the *only* one who matters when you take that last breath.

Don't want for anything but Jesus, daily and in eternity.

FEBRUARY 20

Blessed is the man whose strength is in thee, in
whose heart are the ways of them. (Psalm 84: 5)

With God, your spiritual strength is deep in your heart. Your
strength can overcome the world.

You must talk to God daily in prayer or meditation. Develop
a personal relationship—just *you* and *God*.

FEBRUARY 21

For which cause I also suffer these things, neverless I am not ashamed; for I know whom I have believed and am persuaded that he is able to keep that which I have committed unto him against that day. (2 Timothy 1:2)

I've never met anyone who regretted giving his or her life to Christ. Neither will you.

In God we trust! Commit to him for eternity.

FEBRUARY 22

My flesh and my heart faileth; but God is the strength of my heart and my portion forever. (Psalm 73:26)

We all are aging every day—everyone!

Your body will fail you as it wears out or is attacked by disease or evil, careless times. But God is with you, ready to care for you on earth and for eternity.

Go to him for comfort and peace.

Trust *him*.

FEBRUARY 23

But it is good for me to draw near to God; I have put my trust in the Lord God, that I may declare all thy works. (Psalm 73:28)

It's a great feeling to tell others what God has done in your life. Have you realized the times he has protected you, given you help, kept you from harm, and given you the blessings of a new life, family, jobs, new opportunities, or new friends, neighbors, or coworkers?

God does it all. Pay attention, and watch God work in your life better than you could *ever* imagine.

FEBRUARY 24

The angel of the Lord encampeth round about
them that fear him, and delivereth them. (Psalm
34:7)

Pray for protection—just do it! Pray for yourself. Pray for your
family. Pray when you are full of fear.
God will deliver if you pray.
Trust God. He is in control.

FEBRUARY 25

Casting all your care upon him; for he careth for
you. (1 Peter 5:7, emphasis added)

Don't ever doubt that God cares. Look around. He cares for the
earth and *everything* in it, and that includes *you*.

Have you given him a chance? Talk to God. Keep praying,
and don't quit.

Look, listen, and watch. Read the Bible.

He *will* show you signs, and he does care.

In God we trust.

FEBRUARY 26

Jesus answered and said unto to him [and you],
Verily, verily, I say unto thee, Except a man be
born again, he cannot see the Kingdom of God.
(John 3:30)

You must be born in a spiritual birth and accept Jesus as your
Savior. That is the one and only way to the kingdom of God. You
can't just be good, honest, helpful, and giving. These qualities
will not get you into heaven.

Talk to God, and pray for guidance and forgiveness to accept
Jesus. Now is the time to live for Jesus!

FEBRUARY 27

> But thank be to God, Which giveth us the Victory,
> through our Lord Jesus Christ. (1 Corinthians
> 15:57)

Thank you, God, for your son, Jesus. Without Jesus, I would have no eternal hope or security.

Thank you, God, for your love that is just for *me*. Thank you for being with me, twenty-four/seven.

Thank you for never leaving or giving up on me.

Thank you for heaven, where my soul/spirit will go to live/retire with you and my family and friends for all eternity.

We will have victory!

Come join me.

FEBRUARY 28

> Jesus said unto her, I am the resurrection and
> the life; he that believeth in me, though he were
> dead, yet shall he live. And whosoever liveth and
> believeth in me, shall never die. Believest thou
> this? (John 11:25–26)

There it is again. Read the Bible. Jesus wants you to be saved. He wants you to have eternal life!

If you haven't been saved, it's time. You have no promise of tomorrow or another time. Your soul will live forever. Confess and believe in Jesus.

If you have already accepted Jesus as your Savior, are you living like it? If not, you may not be saved! Think about that.

You can't be a part-time Christian. It's a full- time commitment!

MARCH 1

But he knoweth the way that I take: when he hath tried me, I shall come forth as gold. (Job 23:10)

Trials, worries, problems, stress, and anxiety come into everyone's lives—no exception!

You are not alone. God is with you through it all. Give it all to God.

Have patience and faith in God. He will be with you. You need to trust totally in him. Don't just say it but truly believe, as Jesus did.

In God we trust!

MARCH 2

As for man, his days are as grass: as a flower of
the field, so he flourisheth. (Psalm 103:15)

Spring is a beautiful time of year. Everything is new and fresh.
There is new life and new growth in nature all around us; there
are large and small signs.

God uses this to remind us that we too are a part of nature
and God's plan. He wants us to flourish, to live life to its fullness.
We are here for only a season. Spring, summer, fall, winter—our
lives.

MARCH 3

The Lord is my rock, and my fortress, and my deliverer: my God my strength, in whom I will trust. (Psalm 18:2)

What a statement! What a fact! What a joy to have God—my strength, comfort, peace, fortress, deliverer, and *my rock*!

Thank you, God! Because of you, I will live and survive until you bring me home to heaven.

MARCH 4

Jesus said:

> If ye abide in me, and my words abide in you, ye
> shall ask what ye will, and it shall be done unto
> you. (John 15:7)

Jesus said! Take him at his word! Believe in him! He tells you to ask.

You must abide (accept) Jesus first. Jesus is the *only* answer, the *only* way!

Ask him into your heart and life today. Watch your life change; watch for a peace and comfort in hard, tough times and trials.

MARCH 5

Jesus said:

> Herein is my Father glorified, that ye bear much
> fruit: so shall ye be My disciples. (John 15:8)

Jesus wants you to be successful. Follow his example and be a disciple, a leader, a teacher, a role model, a Christian—twenty-four/seven.

MARCH 6

Jesus said:

> As the Father hath loved me, so have I loved you;
> continue ye in my love. (John 15:9)

Love: an intense feeling of deep affection.

Jesus knew that God loved him. He wants to love you the way God loves. He wants you to love others the way God loved him and he loves you.

It's simple: nothing is better than love. Try it today and every day.

Love like God.

MARCH 7

Jesus said:

> If you keep my commandments, ye shall abide in my love; even as I have kept my Father's commandment, and abide in his love. (John 15:10)

1. Thou shalt have no other gods before me.
2. Thou shalt not make unto thee any graven image.
3. Thou shalt not take the name of the LORD thy God in vain.
4. Remember the Sabbath day, to keep it holy.
5. Honour thy father and thy mother.
6. Thou shalt not kill.
7. Thou shalt not commit adultery.
8. Thou shalt not steal.
9. Thou shalt not bear false witness against thy neighbor.
10. Thou shalt not covet thy neighbor.

Obey these, and you will feel God's love and blessings.

MARCH 8

Jesus said:

> These things have I spoken unto you, that my
> joy might remain in you, and that your joy might
> be full. (John 15:11)

Jesus wants the best for you. He wants you to accept him as your Savior. He wants you to live the way God has shown you, over and over, in the Bible. Real joy comes from living Jesus's example. Earthly joy does not last. He is the true, everlasting, real joy.

MARCH 9

Jesus said:

> This is my commandment, that ye love one
> another, as I have loved you. (John 15:12)

That's tough! Loving one another—people with different opinions; people who are rude, mean, or outspoken; people from different cultures; people with different skin color, different beliefs, different religions—that's tough. But that's what Jesus did, and that's what Jesus expects.

God loves you, and he loves them.

Let God handle the earthly divide. You are not the judge! Show love.

MARCH 10

Jesus said:

> Greater love hath no man than this, that a man
> lay down his life for his friends. (John 15:13)

I can't imagine a friend, relative, coworker, or neighbor dying for me.

Stop—can you imagine someone dying for you?

Thank you, Jesus!

MARCH 11

Hear, O Lord, and have mercy upon me: Lord,
be thou my helper. (Psalm 30:10)

I feel so alone and helpless at times, but I have to stop and
remember that I am not alone—not *ever.*

God is with me! He has and will help me in all situations
and with all problems.

MARCH 12

O Lord thou has brought up my soul from the
grave; thou hast kept me alive, that I should not
go down to the pit. (Psalm 30:3)

So many of our problems are problems that we have brought
on ourselves. We look for a quick fix or quick happiness. We go
to humans, relationships, drugs, and alcohol to try to fulfill our
souls. None of that works and will lead us to sadness, failure
and hopelessness. We dig our own graves!

But the Lord has and will bring you back alive.

MARCH 13

Into thine hand I commit my spirit: thou hast
redeemed me. O Lord God of truth. (Psalm 31:5)

Thank you, Lord, for taking me into your care. Thank you for
redeeming me. Thank you for leading me to the real truth.
My spirit is at peace with you, Lord.

MARCH 14

Who comforteth us in all our tribulation, that we may Be able to comfort them which are in any trouble by the comfort wherewith we ourselves are comforted of God. (2 Corinthians 1:4)

Experience with death comes to everyone. Death happens!

Christians turn to God for comfort and peace. Without God, there is no comfort, no peace! Turn to God. Give your sorrows to him, and look to heaven.

MARCH 15

From the rising of the sun unto the going down
of the same the Lord's name is to be praised.
(Psalm 113:3)

Thank you, God, for the greeting you give with the rising sun.
The sun has not changed. The sun is bright, even in the darkest
storm.

Thank you, God!

MARCH 16

But my God shall supply *all* your need according
to his riches in Glory by Christ Jesus. (Philippians
4:19, emphasis added)

God answers every true petition. In Jesus's own words, he
promised, "If you abide in me, and My words abide in You, you
will ask what you desire, and it shall be done for you" (John
15:7).

In God we trust—with patience and faith.

MARCH 17

The Lord is good unto them that wait for him, to the soul that seekth him. It is good that a man should both hope and quietly wait for the salvation of the Lord. (Lamentations 3:25–26)

Waiting and praying. Waiting and praying. We have to leave it completely in God's hands.

Minutes, hours, days, weeks, months, and years—I've seen God answer prayers in all time frames.

Pray continually. Trust God.

MARCH 18

For as in Adam *all* die, even so in Christ shall all
be made alive. (1 Corinthians 15:22, emphasis
added)

Thank you, Jesus Christ. When I die, my soul will be made alive.

Without Jesus, you have no hope, no peace, and no comfort.
Let your family know that you *know* Jesus. It's an eternal peace
and comfort to everyone.

MARCH 19

For God so loved the world [you], that he gave
his only begotten Son that whosoever believeth
in him should not perish, but have everlasting
life. (John 3:16)

God has *everlasting* life for your soul (spirit) after you die.

Everyone is going to die, even you. Give your heart and
soul to God.

MARCH 20

For all have sinned and come short of the Glory
of God. (Romans 3:23)

No one—not one person—is perfect.

God forgives everyone of everything.

Talk to God daily, anywhere and at any time, twenty-four/
seven. He forgives and wants you to feel his love and comfort
at all times.

MARCH 21

For whosoever shall call upon the name of the
Lord shall be saved. (Romans 10:13)

Peace is only found with God. God can save you now—no
waiting, no delay. Just ask him to come into your heart and save
you. Feel his love, comfort, and peace.

In God we trust.

Share with others—family, friends, coworkers, neighbors—
and let those in your community see Jesus in you.

MARCH 22

Draw near to God, and he will draw nigh to you.
(James 4:8)

He is here, he is there, he is everywhere! You can't be without God. Feel his presence in your life, twenty-four/seven.

MARCH 23

Humble yourselves in the sight of the Lord, and
hehall lift you up. (James 4:10)

My grandmother Mama Rose would always say, "Don't be
proud." She was a strong, humble, dedicated-to-God Christian
woman. She believed and lived God's Word.

Be humble. God is the only one who matters. He has all
power to lift you up.

What does God see in *you*?

MARCH 24

Whereas ye know not what shall be on the morrow. For what is your life? It is even a vapor, that appearth for a little time, and then vanisheth away. (James 4:14)

The devil wants you to worry about tomorrow, your future! It gives Satan great pleasure when you worry.

I once heard a preacher say, "It's a sin to worry."

Why? Because God is in control. In God we must trust—today, tomorrow, and for our future!

MARCH 25

The Lord shall reign for ever and ever. (Exodus
15:18)

What a promise, what peace, what a comfort! God is forever
and ever!

Thank you, Lord. You're the one I can always count on to
be with me, as a hardworking person, and with my precious
family. In God we trust faithfully and daily.

Surely goodness and mercy shall follow me all
the days of my life: and I will dwell in the house
of the lord for ever.

—Psalm 23:6

MARCH 26

Every word of God is pure: he is a shield unto
them that put their *trust* in him. (Proverbs 30:5,
emphasis added)

Read the Bible! Believe it; it's from God to you. Find time to read
the Bible and pray.

Start each day by talking to God. Start off by thanking him.
Name people and things for which you are thankful in your life.

Then, ask for the things you need (not the things you want).
Give it all to God each day.
In God we trust!

MARCH 27

Jesus said:

> Verily, verily, I say unto you, He that hearth
> my word, and believeth on him that sent me,
> hath *everlasting* life, and shall not come into
> condemnation; but is passed from death unto
> life. (John 5:24, emphasis added)

Do you want everlasting life? Do you want it for your family?
Turn to Jesus.
Turn your life from dying and death to *eternal life.*

MARCH 28

Let us therefore come boldly unto the throne of
grace, that we may obtain mercy, and find grace
to help in time of need. (Hebrews 4:16)

The above verse from Hebrews is about prayer. Always
pray—always.

God always answers the prayers of his children, but his
answer isn't always *yes*. Sometimes, his answer is *no* or *wait*.
All are in God's plan just for you.

God knows what is best for us.

Have patience and trust.

MARCH 29

Jesus said:

> But lay up for yourselves treasures in heaven,
> where neither moth nor rust doth corrupt, and
> where thieves do not break through nor steal.
> (Matthew 6:20)

You can't take anything with you when you die. Everyone
will die—*everyone*.

With Jesus, your treasures are waiting in heaven.

MARCH 30

Forever O, Lord, thy word is settled in heaven.
(Psalm 119:89)

The Reverend Billy Graham once said, "God has two textbooks." One is the textbook of nature; by looking at the world, we can learn something about its Creator. The other is the textbook of revelation—the Bible.

God has spoken.

Study those two textbooks!

MARCH 31

Wherefore comfort yourselves together, and edify one another, even as also ye do. (1 Thessalonians 5:11)

Death comes to everyone at any age and at any time. We see and experience the death of family, friends, coworkers, and neighbors.

Hope, peace, and comfort can be given to Christians only from God.

If there's no God, there's no salvation, no peace, no comfort, and no hope.

APRIL 1

For our heart shall rejoice in him, because we
have *trusted* in his holy name. (Psalm 33:21,
emphasis added)

Rejoice means to "feel or show great joy or delight." God wants
you to rejoice when you wake up in the morning and when you
go to bed at night. Rejoice! Be thankful, and trust God with and
in everything every day!

We say, "In God we trust," and we should mean it—no
fooling around, trying to take care of stuff by ourselves.

APRIL 2

I sought the LORD, and he heard me, and delivered me from all my fears. (Psalm 34:4)

I've prayed many, *many* times when I was afraid for myself, my children, my grandchildren, my family, or my friends, community, country, or world. I've *prayed*!

God didn't answer all my prayers, but he heard all of them. He did provide a peace that it was all in his hands and that he was in control. Thank you, Lord.

I couldn't get that assurance from anyone or anything else in this world.

APRIL 3

Jesus said:

> Ask, and it shall be given you; *seek*, and ye shall
> find; knock, and it shall be opened unto you:
> (Matthew 7:7, emphasis added)

Jesus meant these words in Matthew 7:7. *You* have to go through Jesus to find the answers. You cannot find, by yourself, the answers that you seek by your earthly values or wants.

Seek Jesus for *real* answers.

APRIL 4

Jesus said:

> Teaching them to observe ALL things whatsoever
> I have commanded you; and lo, I am *with* you
> always, even unto the end of the world. Amen
> (Matthew 28:20, emphasis added)

Thank you, Jesus! I will *never* be alone. *You* are with me. I can live in peace and feel your comfort every day for the rest of my life!

APRIL 5

And all that believed were *together*, and had all
things common. (Acts 2:44, emphasis added)

When you are with people who believe in Jesus, you have a
bond with each other. You share the peace, comfort, and love
that only believers in Jesus have, daily and for eternity. Choose
your friends based on who you want to lift you up to God's
standards, not on their earthly ideas or standards.

Be a godly example to everyone. Let Jesus shine in *you*.

APRIL 6

And immediately Jesus stretched forth his hand, and caught him, and said unto him, "O thou of little faith, wherefore didst thou doubt?" (Matthew 14:31)

Everyone has had a weak faith at one time; everyone has had doubts.

But Jesus reassures us to have faith in him. He has proven over and over—in my life and in yours—that he loves us and wants us to trust in him for every situation, every day.

Have no doubts. You have Jesus!

APRIL 7

And they that be wise shall shine as the
brightness of the firmament; and they that turn
righteousness as the stars for ever and ever.
(Daniel 12:3)

Work to be wise. Pray daily. Read the Bible daily. Work to gain
heavenly wisdom. Grow daily with God's guidance in all things.
Wisdom will come, and you will *shine*.

My grandmother was an example of Christian wisdom and
righteousness. She was born on April 7, 1895. May this honor
her Christian legacy.

Will you be an example for others too?

APRIL 8

But the path of the just is as the shining light, that shineth more and more unto the perfect day. The way of the wicked is as darkness: they know not at what they stumble. (Proverbs 4:18–19)

What path are you on today? Are you on a lighted path because you are a Christian? Are you trying to live a life that is pleasing to God as you obey God? Is Jesus your Savior, making you a lighted blessing to others?

Are you on a dark, doom-and-gloom path? Are you stumbling on your self-made problems or the problems of others because you were following and not leading? Can you not see because you have darkness all around without Jesus?

Choose Jesus for your light. He is an eternal light. He can change darkness into light.

APRIL 9

Then shall the righteous shine forth as the sun
in the Kingdom of their Father, Who hath ears
to hear, let him hear. (Matthew 13:43)

God needs you to hear his promises, his instruction, and his
guidance in the world and in and around you today. He left you
the Bible for complete instructions.

He wants you to be in his light and not dwell in darkness.
His kingdom is for you.

Choose God and his eternal light—today!

APRIL 10

My brethren count it all joy when ye fall into
divers temptations: Knowing this, that the trying
of your faith worketh patience. (James 1:2–3)

Christians deal with temptations every day. Big and small
temptations are always in front of you. Put your whole heart
and faith in God. Ask for help, and know that he is with you.

He wants you to be patient in all things. That's easy to say
but hard to do, especially if you are someone who wants to do
and fix things *now*. Stop and remember that God's timing is the
best for you, like it or not. God timing is perfect.

APRIL 11

Let the mercy, O LORD, be upon us, according as
we hope in thee. (Psalm 33:22)

Lord, have mercy on all of us. We are not good enough, smart
enough, wise enough, clever enough, or talented enough to
save our own souls. We all need God's mercy and love to give
us peace, comfort, and eternal salvation.

Thank you, Lord, for your daily and eternal mercy.

APRIL 12

Keep thy tongue from evil, and thy lips from speaking guile. Depart from evil, and do good; seek peace, and pursue it. (Psalm 34:13–14)

What wise instructions! Just do it!

Make it a daily habit to let only good, positive words come from your lips. Get out of things that are evil! Look and work to do good daily. Work to bring peace to all situations.

It feels so good to do the right thing in all situations. Watch how your life changes when you follow God's instruction.

APRIL 13

Many are the afflictions of the righteous; but the LORD delivereth him out of them all. (Psalm 34:19)

The word *affliction* means something that causes pain or suffering.

Everyone has many afflictions, even the righteous, even you.

But God is with you. He promises to deliver you out of them all, but it will be his timing, not yours.

In God we trust!

APRIL 14

I laid me down and slept; I awaked: for the LORD
sustained me. (Psalm 3:5)

The word *sustain* means to strengthen or support, physically
or mentally.

Thank you, God, for the many blessings you have given me.
Thank you, Lord, for peace over me as I sleep.

Did you pray before you went to bed? As children, our
prayer was:

Now I lay me down to sleep,
I pray the Lord, my soul to keep.
If I should die before I wake,
I pray the Lord, my soul to take.

It's a simple prayer but very powerful. It's also a prayer you
can pray as an adult. I know several people who died in their
sleep. My dad was one.

Please *pray*!

APRIL 15

But as for me, my prayer is unto thee O Lord, in
an acceptable time; O God, in the multitude of
thy mercy hear me, in the truth of thy salvation.
(Psalm 69:13)

Pray often. In the morning, before you get out of bed, thank
God for the day ahead. Pray while in the car, bus, or train, while
going to work or school. Pray in a moment of silence, wherever
you are.

Pray a prayer of thanks for the food you have to eat, no
matter how much or how little. Pray when help is needed. Pray
a prayer of thanks for your many, many blessings.

Pray at night when you lie down.

Pray *often*!

APRIL 16

Ye are the light of the world. ... Let your light
so shine before men, that they may see your
good works, and glorify your Father which is in
heaven. (Matthew 5:14, 16)

Shine! Show a Christian glow. Let your light shine daily.

Even when nothing seems to be going right and troubles
seem everywhere, be assured by God's promise that he is in
control.

Let your light shine, with God's help, to overcome all other
darkness.

Heaven is glowing—no darkness there!

APRIL 17

Then Jesus said, "Come to me, all of you who are weary and carry heavy burdens, and I will give you rest." (Matthew 11:28)

Oh, I get so tired from work, daily burdens, and problems with people and situations. The stress of all burdens weighs down my body, mind, and soul, but thank you, Jesus, for the rest that only *you* can give!

APRIL 18

My soul, wait thou only upon God; for my
expectation is from him. (Psalm 62:5)

My soul will *never* die. It is waiting for God to release it from my
earthly body. It is his timing and my expectation.

In God we trust!

APRIL 19

For to me to live *is* Christ, and to die is gain.
(Philippians 1:21, emphasis added)

It's a win/win. We win by living daily with Christ, and then we win when we die and gain eternity in heaven.

To die is to gain. *Gain* means to obtain or secure something desired, favorable, or profitable—heaven!

Pray that you will *gain* when you die.

APRIL 20

Teach me to do thy will: for thou art my God:
thy spirit is good: lead me into the land of
uprightness. (Psalm 143:10)

God is working to teach you. He is your God! He will lead your
spirit.
Do your part and follow him daily.
In God you must trust—*daily.*

For God so loved the world, that he gave his only
begotten Son, that whosoever believeth in him
should not perish, but have everlasting life.
—John 3:16

Thank you, Jesus!
Everlasting life is waiting.

APRIL 21

Pray without ceasing. (1 Thessalonians 5:17)

Don't quit. Don't stop. Keep praying! God *is* with you.

Pray, pray, pray—when you get up, during the day, when walking or driving, anywhere and everywhere!

Pray when you go to bed. Ask for your needs, and give thanks for what you have. Pray every day.

Pray without ceasing!

APRIL 22

> In everything give thanks: for this is the *will* of God in Christ Jesus concerning *you.*_(1 Thessalonians 5:18, emphasis added)

It's hard to give thanks for everything.

Sometimes I don't like what is happening to me, but thank you, God, for being with me and taking care of me, even though I don't understand.

If you look back at a horrible failure or disappointment in your life, God had a plan for you. He loves you. He sees and goes before you. God cares about everything that concerns you.

Give thanks!

In God we trust everything!

APRIL 23

Pray for us: for we trust we have a good conscience, in all things willing to live honestly. (Hebrews 13:18)

With God, you will live with a good conscience, Living honestly pleases God and makes you feel good about yourself.

Keep praying to please God, *not* Satan.

APRIL 24

Likewise the spirit also helpeth our infirmities:
for we know not what we should pray for as we
ought: but the Spirit itself maketh intercession
for us with groanings which cannot be uttered.
(Romans 8:26)

Infirmities are physical or mental weaknesses. Sometimes it's
too much—life, problems, stress, depression.

The Holy Spirit is there for you, within you. Give God the
things you cannot control or handle.

In God we trust

APRIL 25

And be not conformed to this world: but be ye transformed by renewing of your mind, that ye may prove what is that good and acceptable, and perfect, will of God. (Romans 12:2)

You will never, *never* be happy by trying to please the world or to be like the world. Be transformed to whatever God's plans are—just for *you*!

APRIL 26

Jesus said:

> Ask, and it shall be given you; seek, and ye shall
> find; knock, and it shall be opened unto you.
> (Matthew 7:7)

Jesus always wants what is best for you. Turn to Jesus for all your help and needs (not wants).

God is always listening, twenty-four/seven. He's always available.

APRIL 27

Jesus said:

> But seek ye *first* the kingdom of God, and his
> righteousness; and all these things shall be
> added unto you. (Matthew 6:33, emphasis
> added)

Jesus said "first"; that means before everything. Before you start your day, before you try to do it yourself, seek *first* the kingdom of God.

In God we trust!

APRIL 28

That *whosoever believeth in him* should not perish, but have *eternal life.*_For God so loved the world, that he gave his only begotten Son, that *whosoever believeth in him should not perish, but have everlasting life.* (John 3:15–16, emphasis added)

You are "whosoever"! You are the one God loves. You are the *one!* The only requirement in these two verses is this: "believeth in him" that you will have eternal life, everlasting life!

Believe: in God we trust.

APRIL 29

In Luke 12:21–34, Jesus tells the story, "God Provides Needs."
Jesus said:

> So is he that layeth up treasure for himself, and
> is *not* rich toward God. (Luke 12:21, emphasis
> added)

Jesus told stories and parables; he taught lessons and gave examples so everyone could understand the daily challenges we face in life. Jesus wants us to feel and see the things that will guide us to the kingdom of God.
Trust God for the things we need.

APRIL 30

It is God that girdeth me with strength, and maketh my way perfect. (Psalm 18:32)

Girdeth means work. God gives strength; he works in me! In God we trust. It doesn't get better than God's perfection.

God will always work for and with you.

MAY 1

The spirit itself beareth witness with *our* spirit, that *we are* the children of God. (Romans 8:16, emphasis added)

Do you feel God's Holy Spirit? Do you feel your spirit within you? This is when we know we are the children of God.

Death comes when our spirits leave our bodies and join God in heaven.

My spirit will *never* get old or die. What a day of rejoicing that will be.

MAY 2

The fear of man bringeth a snare: but whoso putteth his trust in the LORD shall be safe. (Proverbs 29:25)

Fears are everywhere in everything. Give any fear to God, our Lord. God loves you and can calm your fears.

Trust in the Lord.

MAY 3

In God I will praise his word, in God I have put
my trust: I will not fear what flesh can do unto
me. (Psalm 56:4)

Praise God daily. Be thankful daily. Things of the flesh are
temporary. God is eternity, everlasting glory for your soul.
   I will put my trust in God!

MAY 4

What time I am afraid, I will trust in thee. (Psalm
56:3)

Fear will come in so many ways. That's why the above verse is
one of my favorites—and it's short and easy to memorize! This
verse may pop up in your mind at just the right time. In God I
will trust!

MAY 5

That if thou shalt confess with thy mouth the Lord Jesus, and shalt *believe* in thine *heart* that God hath raised him from the dead, *thou shalt be saved.* (Romans 10:9)

Have you confessed? Do you believe in the Lord Jesus? Do you believe with your heart that Jesus was raised from the dead?

You shall be *saved.*

Go live your life with God living inside you. Go into each day with confidence that God is with you.

In God we trust!

MAY 6

The angel of the Lord encampeth roud about
them that fear him, and delivereth them. (Psalm
34:7)

It is so hard to visit individuals in a nursing home or in a hospital
who want to go home but who never will go home again—so
sad. I have to remind myself that I can't change the conditions,
but I have to trust God, with his angels, to watch over and care
for them until they go to their eternal home.

Lord, please bring comfort and peace to the helpless people
all around the world.

MAY 7

But the word of the Lord endureth forever. And this is the word which by the gospel is preached unto you. (1 Peter 1:25)

God gave us a written promise (the Bible) and physical proof (Jesus) that he is with us and he "endureth forever."

He is with us twenty-four/seven.

Thank you, Lord Jesus!

MAY 8

Thy mercy, O Lord, is in the heavens: and thy faithfulness reacheth unto the clouds. (Psalm 36:5)

I love the bright blue sky with white clouds of all shapes and sizes. Pause, look up, enjoy. God is with you. His faithfulness reaches out to you.

MAY 9

Trust in him at all times; ye people, pour out
your heart before him: God is a refuge for us.
(Psalm 62:8)

I heard another tornado warning, then sirens sounding. Time
to take cover.

There are many storms, natural disasters, and impending
dangers. Take refuge with God every time. Trust him in *every*
situation.

MAY 10

Cast thy burden upon the Lord, and he shall sustain thee; he shall never suffer the righteous to be moved. (Psalm 55:22)

It seems that when I'm relieved of one burden, another one follows. I feel overwhelmed as I try to take care of my burdens, as well as caring for my family, friends, community, and country.

As a Christian, I find help when I turn it all over to the Lord.

MAY 11

From the end of the earth will I cry unto thee,
when my heart is over whelmed: lead me to the
rock that is higher than I. (Psalm 61:2)

God will lead you. God will lift you out of situations. He will help you.

Having patience is hard, but it's important to trust God. It's all in his timing, not yours.

MAY 12

Have not I commanded thee? Be strong and of a good courage: be not afraid, neither be thou dismayed: for the LORD the God is with thee whithersoever thou goest. (Joshua 1:9)

Remind yourself daily:

I am strong!

I have courage because I have the Lord God over me and with me!

He is the Almighty!

MAY 13

So that we may boldly say, The LORD is my helper
and I will not fear what man shall do unto me.
(Hebrews 13:6)

When I read the above verse, I thought of all the soldiers,
missionaries, and Christians who faced death, torture, and
abuse by enemies of all sorts.

This was their *only* source to remind them that their God
was there when they faced death and harm.

MAY 14

My voice shalt thou hear in the morning, O Lord;
in the morning will I direct my prayer unto thee
and will look up. (Psalm 5:3)

Before you start your day, before you get out of bed, before your
feet hit the floor, *pray*. Let God hear your voice. Be thankful. Ask
for help and guidance for the day.

Look up and get up. Be thankful—every day.

MAY 15

Now unto him that is able to do exceeding
abundantly above all that we ask or think,
according to the *power* that worketh in us.
(Ephesians 3:20, emphasis added)

God listens. He watches us and loves us.

God is power—amazing power! He is able to answer our
prayers, abundantly and better that we ever could imagine.

Pray daily. Talk to God!

In every trial you ever face, God is in control. You will not
encounter one problem that he can't fix!

MAY 16

The fear of the LORD is the beginning of knowledge: but fools despise wisdom and instruction. (Proverbs 1:7)

Who wants to be a fool? Who denies God's power? Who is afraid to die, and why?

Have you gained the knowledge to gain God's instruction? If not, start today to gain knowledge about God and his plan for you.

In God we trust.

MAY 17

So that thou incline thine ear unto wisdom,
and apply thine heart to understanding.
(Proverbs 2:2)

God is looking for people who want to gain wisdom. He
wants your heart to feel his presence; he wants you to gain
understanding.

Read your Bible daily, and look for answers.

Are you listening?

MAY 18

My help cometh from the Lord which made heaven and earth. (Psalm 121:2)

How powerful! How amazing is God's power! He's the Almighty! He's a help in all times and all situations for all people! In God we trust.

MAY 19

Unto thee lift, I up mine eyes, O thou that
dwellest in the heavens. (Psalm 123)

Look up to the brilliant, bright-blue sky. Look up into the mighty,
massive storm clouds. Look up to the amazing twinkling stars,
moon, and planets at night.

God dwellest in the heavens!

We are all so blessed that he gives us a reminder and shows
us his creations daily!

MAY 20

Then shall ye call upon me and ye shall go and pray unto me, and I will hearken unto you. And ye shall seek me, and find me, when ye shall search for me with *all* your heart. (Jeremiah 29:12–13, emphasis added)

Prayer must be a part of your life. There's nothing better than praying to God each day—*multiple times* each day.

You don't have to speak your prayers out loud. Talk to God with your heart.

Call upon God. He's waiting on you.

MAY 21

Jesus said:

> I am come a light into the world, that whosoever
> believeth on me should not abide in darkness.
> (John 12:46)

Darkness holds the unknown, the unseen; there is fear in not knowing what is ahead.

Thank you, Jesus, for the light you give. Your brightness gives us hope, comfort, and peace.

Go toward the light. Jesus is waiting for you. He's your Savior!

MAY 22

I will say of the LORD, He is my refuge and my
fortress: my God: in him will I trust. (Psalm 19:2)

You must believe in God and his power, his promise, and his
Son's sacrifice and death for you. You must believe before you
can trust. Can you say, "I believe"?

I am praying for your soul, that you will accept Jesus and
spend eternity with me. He is my refuge!

MAY 23

The heavens declare the glory of God: and the firmament showeth his handywork. (Psalm 19:1)

God shows you his handywork night and day. Look to the heavens—the stars are his handiwork, as are the blue sky and the clouds.

God is *everywhere.* Look at the amazing the creations of God. You are one of those creations!

MAY 24

Whosoever shall confess that Jesus is the Son of God, God dwelleth in him, and he in God. (1 John 4:15)

Jesus is the Son of God. He is my Savior and my ancestors' Savior. We have confessed that God dwells in our lives and souls.

Pray that your eyes and heart will be opened to see and feel God's power.

MAY 25

Call unto me, and I will answer thee and shew
thee great and mighty things, which thou
knowest not. (Jeremiah 33:3)

God promises to answer and to show for us. He is mighty;
we cannot know his almighty power. He is mightier than our
earthly bodies and minds can understand.

In God we trust!

MAY 26

No weapon that is formed against thee shall
prosper: and every tongue, that shall rise against
thee in judgement thou shalt condemn. This is
the heritage of the servants of the LORD, and
their righteousness is of me, saith the LORD.
(Isaiah 54:17)

The blessing of being God's servant and being comforted by
the heritage of the Lord is an amazing gift to all who believe.
God's promise and love is a daily gift.
Thank you, Lord!

MAY 27

For he shall give his angels charge over thee,
To keep thee in all ways. (Psalm 19:11)

Thank you, God, for the angels of protection, security, and safety.

I have felt the angels in charge over me. I have prayed for angels to surround my family members, my church family, schoolchildren, and friends.

In God I trust!

MAY 28

For the kingdom of God is not in word, but in power. (1 Corinthians 4:20)

God shows his power daily. He is the Almighty and the Creator. There is nothing that God can't do.

In God *we must* trust.

MAY 29

We are troubled on every side, yet not distressed: we are perplexed, but not in despair. (2 Corinthians 4:8)

Thank you, God. The above are earthly problems. They will pass, and you will be with us every second of every day. God, you provide so much needed comfort and peace.

I give *all* my trials and problems to you, my Lord.

MAY 30

Who by him do believe in God, that raised him
up from the dead and gave him glory; that your
faith and hope might be in God. (1 Peter 1:21)

I can trust God in life and in death. The Bible tells me so.

God wants me to turn to him in all situations. My faith and
hope grow with each new situation I face. I have confidence
that God will take care of me, as he does with the entire world.

MAY 31

And even to your old age, I am he; and even to hoar hairs will I carry you: I have made and I will bear: even I will carry, and will deliver you. (Isaiah 46:4)

It doesn't matter how old or how young you are; God will be there for you. He will carry you though the trials you face in every season of your life. God is not a part-time God. He was with you in the beginning when you were forming in your mother womb. He will be with you even into death. God is with you.

In God we trust our entire lives.

JUNE 1

For God hath not given us the spirit of fear; but of power, and of love, and of a sound mind. (2 Timothy 1:7)

God's power is amazing! God is greater than we can imagine!

JUNE 2

Behold, God is my salvation: I will trust, and not be afraid: for the LORD JEHOVAH is my strength and my song; he also is become my salvation. (Isaiah 12:2)

I *will* trust in God. Will you?

JUNE 3

For I am not ashamed of the gospel of Christ:
for it is the power of God unto salvation to every
one that believeth; to the Jew first, and also to
the Greek. (Romans 1:16)

When you believe, when you trust, then you will feel the power
of God.

You will never be ashamed of God.

JUNE 4

Jesus said, as he looked to heaven:

> As thou hast given him power over all flesh,
> that he should give eternal life to as many as
> tho hast given him. And this is life eternal, that
> they might know thee the *only true God* and
> Jesus Christ, whom thou hast sent. (John 17:2–3,
> emphasis added)

There have been and still continue to be many gods of all kinds.
But there is *only one* true God who offers salvation and eternal
life.

JUNE 5

Wait on the Lord; be of good courage, and he shall strengthen thine heart: wait, I say, on the Lord. (Psalm 27:14)

The Lord's timing is perfect timing. Wait! Trust God.

JUNE 6

Fear thou not I am with thee: be not dismayed;
for I am thy God: I will strengthen thee; yea, I
will help thee; yea, I will uphold thee with the
right hand of my righteousness. (Isaiah 41:10)

God says "I am" and "I will."
 Believe and trust in him.

JUNE 7

And we have known and believed the love that
God hath to us. God is love; and he that dwellth
in love dwellth in God, and God in him. (1 John
4:16)

Thank you, Lord, for your everlasting love. You love us
twenty-four/seven.

JUNE 8

Who is among you that feareth the Lord, that
obeyeth the voice of his servant, that walketh
in darkness, and hath no light? Let him <u>trust</u> in
the name of the Lord, and stay upon his God.
(Isaiah 50:10)

Darkness is full of the unseen and the unknown.
Trust in the Lord. You are *never* alone!

JUNE 9

God is our refuge and strength, a very present
help in trouble. (Psalm 46:1)

God *is* with us. God *is* our strength. God helps us.
In God we trust.

JUNE 10

But of him are ye in Christ Jesus, who of God is made unto us wisdom, and righteousness, and sanctification, and redemption. That, according as it is written; He that glorieth, let him glory in the Lord. (1 Corinthians 1:30–31)

No one knows it all, but we have *access* to knowledge and wisdom in the Bible.

JUNE 11

For who hath known the mind of the Lord, that
he may instruct him? But we have the mind of
Christ. (1 Corinthians 2:16)

Who knows the mind of the Lord? No, not me!

God gives us the living Bible, full of knowledge and wisdom.
Read it. Use it.

JUNE 12

But what saith it? The word is nigh thee, even in thy mouth, and in thy heart: that is, the word of faith, which we preach. (1 Corinthians 2:16)

The Bible is God's gift to you and everyone before you. It's God's word to *you*.

JUNE 13

For whosoever shall call upon the name of the
Lord shall be saved. (Romans 10:13)

"Whosoever" refers to you and me.
Call upon the Lord. He wants *all* to be saved!

JUNE 14

The LORD preserveth the simple: I was brought
low, and he helped me. (Psalm 116:6)

Thank you, Lord, for preserving me. I have had bad days,
hopeless days, and sad days, and you helped me.
 Please let God help you.
 In God we trust!

JUNE 15

Return unto they rest, O my soul: for the Lord
hath dealt bountifully with thee. (Psalm 116:7)

Are you looking for rest for your soul? God has that rest, that
peace, that comfort, which every soul needs.

JUNE 16

Being confident of this very thing, that he which hath begun a good work in you will perform it until the day of Jesus Christ. (Philippians 1:6)

What a promise from God!

JUNE 17

Who is he that overcometh the world, but he that believeth that Jesus is the Son of God? (1 John 1:5)

Believe that Jesus is the Son of God.
Overcome the world!
Do you believe?

JUNE 18

It is of the LORD's mercies that we are not consumed, because his compassions fail not. They are new every morning: great is thy faithfulness. (Lamentations 3:22–23)

God loves us. He shows us daily.

JUNE 19

For the LORD is good; his mercy is everlasting;
and his truth endureth to all generations. (Psalm
100:5)

The above verse is not hard to understand.
    Fact: God is good.
    Fact: He is everlasting.
    Fact: God is true for *all* generations, past and present.

JUNE 20

And in the morning, rising up a great while before day, he went out and departed into a solitary place, and there prayed. (Mark 1:35)

Jesus shows us that prayer is important.

I have a cousin who begins praying at 4:00–5:00 a.m. I begin around 6:00 a.m., or if I wake during the night, or whenever I feel a need to pray.

Prayer is important. Find your time—any time. Pray!

JUNE 21

But as it is written, Eye hath not seen, nor ear heard, neither have entered into the heart of man, the things which God hath prepared for them that love him. (1 Corinthians 2:9)

We humans *cannot* imagine what God has prepared for us. In God we trust!

JUNE 22

For since the beginning of the world men have not heard nor perceived by the ear, neither hath the eye seen O God beside thee what he hath prepared for him that waiteth for him. (Isaiah 64:4)

There is *not* another God!

There's *not* another God who forgives and loves me.

There's *not* another God who answers prayers.

There's *not* another God who give me hope.

There's *not* another God who promises me eternity after death.

JUNE 23

Neither is there salvation in any other: for there
is none other name under heaven given among
me, where by we must be saved. (Acts 4:12)

Jesus is the *only* salvation. There is none other—*only Jesus.*

JUNE 24

Thy sun shall no more go down, neither shall thy moon withdraw itself: for the LORD shall be thine everlasting light and the days of thy mourning shall be ended. (Isaiah 60:20)

God promises everlasting light and no more mourning. Are you ready?

Do you *trust* God?

JUNE 25

Let not your heart be troubled: ye believe in God, believe also in me. In my Father's house are many mansions: if it were not so, I would have told you. I go to prepare a place for You. And if I go and prepare for you, I will come again and receive you unto myself, that where I am, there ye may be also. And whither I go ye know and the way ye know. (John 14:1–4)

Thank you, Jesus. Thank you!

JUNE 26

But now thus saith the LORD that created thee,
O Jacob, and he that formed thee, O Israel, Fear
not: for I have redeemed thee, I have called thee
by thy name; thou art mine. (Isaiah 43:1)

God created you. God knows you by name. Trust him!

JUNE 27

The LORD shall fight for you, and ye shall hold
your peace. (Exodus 14:14)

Let God have your problems. Let God fight for you.
In God you must trust!

JUNE 28

How precious also are thy thoughts unto me O God! How great is the sum of them! If I should count them, they are more in number than the sand: when I awake, I am still with thee. (Psalm 139:17–18)

God loves me more than I can imagine. God thinks of me. God knows what is best for me.

There are a lot of grains of sand, but he is with me always.

JUNE 29

He only is my rock and my salvation: he is my defence; I shall not be moved. (Psalm 62:6)

God is for you and me. God is all you need to face anything. Do not be moved from this. Trust God!

JUNE 30

For the scripture saith unto Pha'raoh, Even for this same purpose have I raised thee up, that I might shew my power in thee, and that my name might be declared throughout all the earth. (Romans 9:17)

God has a reason and purpose for you—just for you. He's teaching us to trust him.

JULY 1

If thou put the brethren in remembrance of these things, thou shalt be a good minister of Jesus Christ, nourished up in the words of faith and of good doctrine whereunto thou hast attained. (1 Timothy 4:6)

You must have faith in God. He has given you the Bible for a sound and good doctrine to guide you in everything.

JULY 2

That in *everything* ye are *enriched* by *faith* by him, in *all utterance*, and in *all knowledge*. (1 Corinthians 1:5, emphasis added)

Cling to God's unchanging hand!

JULY 3

Blessed be God, even the Father of our Lord Jesus Christ, the Father of mercies, and *the God of all comfort.* (2 Corinthians 1:3, emphasis added)

Only God can give "all comfort."

JULY 4

And he said unto me, My grace is sufficient for thee: for my strength is made perfect in weakness. Most gladly therefore will I rather glory in my infirmities, that the power of Christ may rest upon me. Therefore I take pleasure in infirmities in reproaches, in necessities, in persecutions, in distresses for Christ's sake: for when I am weak, then am I strong. (2 Corinthians 12:9–10)

Jesus said, "My grace is sufficient for thee: for my strength is made perfect in weakness."
   Be strong with Jesus.
   Thank you, Jesus!

JULY 5

The Lord <u>liveth</u>; and blessed be *my* rock; and exalted be the God of the rock of my salvation. (2 Samuel 22:47, emphasis added)

Thank you, God, for being my solid and unchanging rock for my soul. You give me peace and comfort in all of life's challenges.

JULY 6

Jesus said, "Heaven and earth shall pass away, but my words shall not pass away. (Matthew 24:35)

God's Word does not change!
Read the Bible!

JULY 7

Jesus said, "Heaven and earth shall pass away: but my words shall not pass away. But of that day and that hour knoweth no man, no, not the angels which are in heaven, neither the Son, but the Father. (Mark 13:31–32)

God is coming, and only he knows the time.
    Are you ready?
    Is your family ready?

I'm ready, and I pray you are too.

JULY 8

The grass whithereth, the flower fadeth: but the
word of our God shall stand forever. (Isaiah 40:8)

God shows us daily and in every season that nothing lasts, but
the Word of God will stand forever. That's a promise from God.
     Read the Bible, the Word of God, and believe *forever.*
     I believe everything in the Bible, from cover to cover. I don't
understand it all, but I *believe* it all.

JULY 9

Behold, I am the LORD, the God of all flesh: is there any thing too hard for me? (Jeremiah 32:27)

Nothing, Lord, nothing is too hard for you. Thank you for reminding me.

Give God your problems.

JULY 10

And he answered, *Fear not*: for they that be with us are *more* than they that be with them. And Elisha *prayed* and said, Lord, I pray the open this eyes, that *he may see*. And the Lord *opened the eyes* of the young man: and *he saw*: and, behold, the mountain was full of horses and chariots of fire round about Elisha. (2 Kings 6:16–17, emphasis added)

It is amazing how God protects us. In God we trust!

JULY 11

I will go before thee and make the crooked places straight: I will break in pieces the gates of brass, and cut in sunder the bars of iron. (Isaiah 45:2)

What a promise from God—that he will always go before us. Thank you, God!

JULY 12

God said:

> Look unto me, and be saved all the ends of
> the earth: for I am God and there is none else.
> (Isaiah 45:22)

You can look for comfort, hope, peace, and salvation but you can *only* find it in God.

Do you believe? Stop and talk to God.

JULY 13

Alas! For that day is great, so that none is like
it: it is even the time of Jacob's trouble: but he
shall be saved out of it. (Jeremiah 30:7)

Read in the Bible about Jacob's life. God was there in every situation.

Trust God. He is with you during all trouble.

JULY 14

Fear thou not: for I am with thee: be not dismayed; for I am thy God: I will strengthen thee: yea, I will help thee; ye, I will uphold thee with the right hand of my righteousness. (Isaiah 41:10)

Thank you, God, for being with me. When I stop, I can feel your strength.

Thank you, God, for all your help with everything that I face daily.

Thank you, God.

JULY 15

There shall not any man be able to stand before thee all the days of thy life: as I was with Moses, so I will be with thee: *I will not fail thee, nor forsake thee.* (Joshua 1:5, emphasis added)

God is with you. Read the Bible. He was always with Moses. He promises to be with you too.

God *is* with you.

JULY 16

But if the Spirit of him that raised up Jesus from
the dead *dwell in you*, he that raised up Christ
from the dead shall also quicken your mortal
bodies by *his Spirit* that *dwelleth in you*. (Romans
8:11, emphasis added)

Amazing! The same God who raised up Jesus is with you. He
will raise your spirit that dwells in you, as he did Jesus.

Thank you, Lord. Thank you for the Spirit inside me. Thank
you for taking my spirit to be with you in heaven when I depart
this mortal body.

Thank you, Jesus, for going before me and making it all
possible.

JULY 17

Be merciful unto me, O God, be merciful unto me: for *My soul trusteth* in thee: yea, in the shadow of thy wings will I make my refuge, until these calamities be overpast. (Psalm 57:1, emphasis added)

Tough times—everyone has them. Let your soul trust God. He will always be your refuge.

This too shall pass.

Thank you, God!

JULY 18

This is the day which the LORD hath made: we
will rejoice and be glad in it. (Psalm 118:24)

Rejoice every day! God doesn't want you to live with doom
and gloom. He wants the best for you. He wants you to see
and appreciate the many blessings that surround you each and
every day.

Be glad that you have God.

JULY 19

Behold, I will do a new thing now it shall spring forth: shall ye not know it? I will even make a way in the wilderness, and rivers in the desert. (Isaiah 43:19)

God can change *any* situation.
    In God we trust!

JULY 20

For I know the thoughts that I think toward you,
saith the Lord, thoughts of peace, and not evil,
to give you and expected end. (Jeremiah 29:11)

With God or without God—it's your choice. You have other
choices too: good or evil, heaven or hell.

God gives you a choice.

God is ready to give you daily blessings.

JULY 21

Being confident of this very thing, that he which hath begun a good work in you will perform it until the day of Jesus Christ. (Philippians 1:6)

Thank you, Lord, for giving us confidence in you and your power in all situations and all challenges.

Thank you, Lord, for giving daily blessings.

Are you ready for Jesus to come?

JULY 21

Jesus said:

> Peace, I leave with you, my peace. I give unto
> you: not as the world giveth, give I unto you.
> Let not your heart be troubled, neither let it be
> afraid. (John 14:27)

Jesus promised. Trust in him.
Thank you, Jesus.

JULY 22

Thy word is a lamp unto my feet, and a light
unto my path. (Psalm 119:105)

Thank you, God, for shining and giving light in our darkness
and leading us out of dark places in our lives.
Thank you for a lighted path to you.

JULY 23

The angel of the Lord encampeth round about them that fear him, and delivereth them. O taste and see that the Lord is good: blessed is the man that trusteth in him. (Psalm 34:7–8, emphasis added)

Trust God. He is almighty over everything.
I love being surrounded by God!

JULY 24

As the hart panteth after the water brooks, so panteth *my soul* after thee, O God. *My soul* thirsteth for God for the living God: when shall I come and appear before God? (Psalm 42:1–2, emphasis added)

My soul needs God. I'm ready for my soul to appear before God. Is your soul ready?

JULY 25

O give thanks unto the LORD, for he is good: for
his mercy endureth for ever. (Psalm 107:1)

Give thanks every day.
　　Start each day and end each day with thanks to God.

JULY 26

Oh that men would praise the LORD for his goodness, and for his wonderful works to the children of men! And let them sacrifice the sacrifices of thanksgiving, and *declare* his works with rejoicing. (Psalm 107:21–22, emphasis added)

Be thankful. Rejoice. Praise God!

JULY 27

Oh that men would praise the Lord for his goodness and for his wonderful works to his children of men! (Psalm 107:31)

Praise God for his goodness and his wonderful works. How blessed we would be if we would appreciate God's blessings that surround us.

Praise God.

Give thanks!

JULY 28

Whoso is wise, and will observe these things,
even they shall understand the loving kindness
of the Lord. (Psalm 107:43)

Observe, look, see, and experience the many, *many* things of
God's loving, giving kindness.
    You must look to be able to see.
    God is with you.

JULY 29

Give us help from trouble: for vain is the help of man. (Psalm 108:12)

In God we trust in times of trouble—and there will be trouble in the life of every person. God is mighty, powerful, and dependable.

JULY 30

Praise ye the LORD. O give thanks unto the LORD; for he is good: for his mercy endureth forever. (Psalm 106:1)

God is forever. Give thanks!
　　After the darkest hour comes the light.

JULY 31

And herein do I exercise myself to have always
a conscience void of offence toward God, and
toward me. (Acts 24:16)

Do you exercise yourself to have a conscience, to work to *not*
to be an offense to God and man?
　It should be a daily exercise for everyone—yes, everyone!

AUGUST 1

And Noah did according unto *all* that the Lᴏʀᴅ *commanded* him. (Genesis 7:5, emphasis added)

Noah obeyed God with everything. Do you do what God commands you to do?

In God, Noah trusted.

> For I the Lᴏʀᴅ thy God will hold thy right hand,
> saying unto thee, *Fear not; I will help thee.*
> —Isaiah 41:13 (emphasis added)

AUGUST 2

And the angel of the Lord called unto him out of heaven and said, Abraham, Abraham; and he said, Here am I. (Genesis 22: 11)

When God calls you, do *you* say, "Here am I"?

AUGUST 3

And when the LORD saw that he turned aside to see, God called unto him out of the midst of the bush, and said, Moses, Moses, And he said, Here am I. (Exodus 3:4)

When God calls you, do you say, "Here am I"? God does call! Do you listen?

AUGUST 4

Ye shall keep my Sabbath, and reverence my
sanctuary: I am the Lord. (Leviticus 26:2)

Find a church home. God has a sanctuary just for you.
　The book of Leviticus is full of the phrase, "And the Lord
spake." Listen to God!

AUGUST 5

If a man vow a vow unto the Lord or swear and oath to bind his soul with a bond: he shall not break his word, he shall do according to all that proceedth out of his mouth. (Numbers 30:2)

My dad always said that a man is as good as his word.

What comes out of your mouth? Is your word good? God expects it to be!

AUGUST 6

But if from thence thou shalt seek the Lord thy
God, thou shalt find him if thou seek him with
all thy heart and with all thy soul. (Deuteronomy
4:29)

God wants your whole heart and soul. Have you given your all
to him?

Where will your soul spend eternity? Only you can choose.

AUGUST 7

That in everything ye are enriched by him, in all knowledge. Even as the testimony of Christ was confirmed in you: So that ye come behind in no gift: waiting for the coming of our Lord Jesus Christ. (1 Corinthians 1:5–7)

I pray that everyone who reads the above verses is waiting for the coming of our Lord Jesus Christ and is waiting with joy, not fear.

If you have fear, it's time to give your life to Jesus.

AUGUST 8

The grace of our Lord Jesus Christ be with you
all. Amen. (Romans 16:24)

Jesus Christ is for you—all of you. No exceptions! *You!*
　You breathe oxygen from the air every day.
　God is like oxygen: you can't see him, but you can't live
without him!

AUGUST 9

Jesus said:

> If any man serve me, let him follow me; and
> where I am, there shall also my servant be; if
> any man serve me, him will *my* Father honor.
> (John 12:26, emphasis added)

Are you a servant to God? Each life will pass, but only what
has been done for Jesus will last.

AUGUST 10

The eyes of the LORD are in every place, beholding
the evil and the good. (Proverbs 15:3)

God is watching us twenty-four/seven.
    Are you doing good or evil? There's no in between.

AUGUST 11

The fear of the Lord prolongeth days: but the years of the wicked shall be shortened. (Proverbs 10:27)

I fear God if I don't obey. Do you?

AUGUST 12

The fear of the LORD is to hate evil: pride and arrogancy, and the evil way, and the froward mouth, do I hate. (Proverbs 8:13)

Lord, I wish to please you, but I have a constant battle with my human nature. I need you to help me to look to you, not to my natural thoughts of this world.

Please let me see, think, and say things that honor you and your biblical teachings. I fear not obeying you daily. Please help me.

AUGUST 13

Then spake Jesus again unto them saying, I am
the light of the world: he that followeth me shall
not walk in darkness, but shall have the light of
life. (John 8:12)

Everyone feels darkness in his or her life. Jesus is the light that
will lead us out of those dark events.

In God we trust.

AUGUST 14

For I the Lord thy God will hold thy right hand,
saying unto thee, Fear not, I will help thee.
(Isaiah 41:13)

God is with you. He's the Almighty. He can handle *all* your fear.
In God we trust.

AUGUST 15

He giveth power to the faint; and to them that have no might he increaseth strength. (Isaiah 40:29)

God is all power. I have felt drained, beaten, defeated, weak, lifeless, and faint, but God has *always* been with me and *always* has given me the strength I need.

You gotta trust God.

AUGUST 16

I will instruct thee and teach thee in the way
which thou shalt go: I will guide thee with mine
eye. (Psalm 32:8)

What a comfort to know that God will guide and show me parts
in the Bible that instruct me in my daily life and future.

I must look—and you must look—for God's guidance and
teaching in the Bible and around us daily.

Thank you, Lord, for the Bible and your patience.

AUGUST 17

For by grace are ye saved through faith; and
that not of yourselves: it is the gift of God.
(Ephesians 2:8)

Salvation is gift of God to you.

Have you been saved—*really* saved? Have you changed your
attitude and your actions so that the Holy Spirit shines in you?
Do you share your gift with others?

Only you can answer those questions.

AUGUST 18

For now we live, if ye stand fast in the LORD. (1
Thessalonians 2:8)

Stand fast with God. That's the *best* of living! Hold your ground
in doing what is right and good. If you do what's right, you will
never be wrong.

AUGUST 19

I can do all things through Christ which strengtheneth me. (Philippians 4:13)

The above verse shows the confidence that only God can give. My strength to handle every challenge comes from Christ.
In God I trust.

AUGUST 20

Giving thanks always for all things unto God and
the Father in the name of our LORD Jesus Christ.
(Ephesians 5:20)

Are you thankful every day for everything?

That word *always* means being thankful even when things
don't work out for you, being thankful for disappointments—
giving thanks *always*.

God has plans for you that you can't see.

In God we trust.

AUGUST 21

Love not the world, neither the things, that are in the world. If any man love the world, the love of the Father is not in him. (1 John 2:15)

God's love is eternal and everlasting. What do you choose: love of the world or the love of God?

The choice is yours.

AUGUST 22

This is a faithful saying, and worthy of all acceptation, that Christ Jesus came into the world to save sinners: of whom I am chief. (1 Timothy 1:15)

Everyone is a sinner. *No one* is perfect. Sin is sin, whether large or small.

Thank you, Jesus, for forgiveness and eternal life.

AUGUST 23

Jesus said:

> He that believeth on me, as the scripture hath
> said, out of his belly shall flow rivers of living
> water. (John 7:38)

When Jesus is your choice and you believe—when you have
total belief—he flows inside and outside of you.

You are full of the Holy Spirit!

AUGUST 24

Thou, even thou, art Lord alone; thou hast made Heaven, the heaven of heavens, with all their host the earth, and all things that are therein, the seas, and all that is there in and thou preservest them all; and the host of heaven worshippeth thee. (Nehemiah 9:6)

God is the Almighty; he is so powerful, more so than anyone on earth can imagine.

In God we trust everything.

AUGUST 25

So teach us to number our days, that we may apply our hearts unto wisdom. (Psalm 90:12)

Oh, to always seek God's wisdom. Let your heart fill with the wisdom that God gives you each day.

AUGUST 26

His lord said unto him, Well done thou good
and faithful servant: thou hast been faithful
over a few things, I will make the ruler over
many things: enter thou into the joy of the Lord.
(Matthew 25:21)

I'm praying to live my life so that God will say, "Well done, my
good and faithful servant!"
   Is that your purpose and goal?

> O Give thanks unto the LORD; call upon his name:
> make known his deeds among the people.
> —Psalm 105:1

AUGUST 27

Jesus said:

> Labour not for the meat which perisheth, but
> for that meat which endureth unto everlasting
> life which the Son of man shall give unto you:
> for him hath God the Father sealed. (John 6:27)

Don't coast through your life without a passion to live for
God. An everlasting life is waiting for you.

AUGUST 28

If my people, which are called by my name, shall humble themselves, and pray, and seek my face, and turn from their wicked ways; then will I hear from heaven, and will forgive their sin, and will heal their land. (2 Chronicles 7:14)

This is God's promise to *all* of us—that he will forgive our sin. Start humble. Stay humble and pray.

AUGUST 29

I laid me down and slept; I awaked; for the Lord
sustained me. (Psalm 3:5)

Thank you, Lord, for every day and every night. Thank you!
Give thanks—it's all God!

AUGUST 30

And this is the confidence that we have in him,
that, if we ask anything according to his will, he
heareth us: (1 John 5:14)

Pray, pray, and pray. God listens and hears. His will is always
what is best for us, whether we like it or not.

Prayer is a blessing.

God is listening. He hears every word.

AUGUST 31

Confess your faults one to another, and pray one
for another, that ye may be healed. The effectual
fervent prayer of a righteous man availeth much.
(James 5:16)

No one is above another person.
Pray with a sincere heart daily.

SEPTEMBER 1

Jesus said:

> And this is the will of him that sent me, that
> everyone which seeth the Son, and believeth on
> him, may have everlasting life; and I will raise
> him up at the last day. (John 6:40)

Everlasting life is offered to everyone. It is what Jesus gives
to you.
    Do you believe?
    Do others see Jesus in *you*?

SEPTEMBER 2

The LORD shall fight for you, and ye shall hold
your peace. (Exodus 14:14)

It's hard *not* to try to fix every disagreement or each conflict,
but God said he would handle it.

Let God fight for you.

In God—not humans—we trust!

> Bless the LORD, O my soul: and all that is within
> me, bless his holy name.
> Bless the LORD, O my soul, and forget not all his
> benefits:
> Who forgiveth all thine iniquities, who healeth
> all they diseases;
>
> —Psalm 103:1–3

SEPTEMBER 3

Jesus said:

> I said therefore unto you, that ye shall die in
> your sins: for if ye believe not that I am he, ye
> shall die in your sins. (John 8:24)

Thank you, Lord Jesus, for dying for my sins. I believe in you.

I *am* thankful.

SEPTEMBER 4

Look not every man on his own things, but every
man also on the things of others. (Philippians 2:4)

Be observers of others. Imagine their worries and problems. Be
kind, helpful, and humble.

SEPTEMBER 5

O LORD, thou hast searched me, and known me.
(Psalm 139:1)

No one knows me like God knows me. He is with me, twenty-four/
seven.

Does he approve of everyone, everything, and every
thought?

Talk it *all* over with God.

SEPTEMBER 6

In God is my salvation and my glory: the rock of my strength, and my refuge, is in God. (Psalm 62:7)

God has been my strength and my refuge when I have faced more than I could handle.

Stop and realize that God is with you *always.*

In God we trust.

SEPTEMBER 7

No man can come to me, except the Father
which hath sent me draw him; and will raise
him up at the last day. (John 6:44)

Jesus, I believe that your Father is my Father too. Just as he
raised you up, he will do the same for me.

Jesus, you are my Savior.

Thank you, Jesus.

SEPTEMBER 8

Verily, verily, I say unto you, He that believeth
on me hath everlasting life. (John 6:47)

What a promise of everlasting life!
   In God we believe and trust.
   Do you have that full trust?

SEPTEMBER 9

Consider what I say; and the Lord give thee
understanding in all things. (2 Timothy 2:7)

I don't understand electricity, phones, TVs, cars, computers, the
internet, and almost everything around me every day. I simply
trust that certain things will work when I need them.

I totally trust God. It's all in faith.

In God we trust.

SEPTEMBER 10

But my God shall supply all your need according to his riches in glory by Christ Jesus. (Philippians 4:19)

Patience—I always need patience.
In God, I have to wait and trust with all things.
He shall supply.

SEPTEMBER 11

The Lord hath prepared his throne in the heavens; and his Kingdom ruleth over all. (Psalm 103:19)

Our Lord does not rule over this or that. He "ruleth over all."
What an amazing promise and power!
Trust God in *everything.*

SEPTEMBER 12

Bless the Lord, O my soul, and forget not *all* his
benefits. (Psalm 103:2, emphasis added)

Oh, my soul, please don't ever forget God's love, power, comfort,
help, security, promises, everlasting life, and never-ending
benefits.

Thank you, Lord.

I want to thank you each day!

SEPTEMBER 13

> Pleasant words are as an honeycomb, sweet to the soul, and health to the bones. (Proverbs 16:24)

You've heard the old saying, "If you can't say something good, don't say anything at all."

God wants you to use words that are good for your soul, that will bring health to you too!

Try to use "pleasant words" today.

SEPTEMBER 14

> If my people, which are called by my name shall
> humble themselves, and pray, and seek my face
> and turn from their wicked ways; then will I
> hear from heaven, and will forgive their sin, and
> will heal their land. (2 Chronicles 7:14)

If is a big word!

God made it simple for people to follow him.

Be humble and pray daily for God to help you, your family,
and our country.

SEPTEMBER 15

The L<small>ORD</small> our God be with us, as he was with our fathers; let him not, leave us, nor forsake us. (1 Kings 8:57)

Grandparents, aunts, uncles, cousins—all these relatives and my forefathers were Christian examples and a Christian influence for me. Past generations had only the King James Bible to read, study, and learn about Jesus.

You don't need fancy translations to learn about Jesus. God will help you understand the Bible if you open your heart and mind. You can feel his Spirit, just as your forefathers did.

SEPTEMBER 16

That he may incline our hearts unto him, to walk
in all his ways and to keep his commandments,
and his statutes, and his judgments, which he
commanded our fathers. (1 Kings 8:58)

God is a God of generations. He wants us to continue as our
forefathers did and read the Bible daily.

Turn to God for everything!

God has *not* changed and his commands have *not* changed
since our forefathers' day. Don't be fooled by evil people who
want to change God's Word to fit their sins.

SEPTEMBER 17

The just man walketh in this integrity; his
children are blessed after him. (Proverbs 20:7)

Integrity is the quality of being honest and having strong moral
principles. This is what God expects from everyone.

Teach and show your children and grandchildren. Show *all*
children. Everyone will be blessed. This will please God. Be a
blessing to others.

SEPTEMBER 18

Bear ye one another's burdens, and so fulfill the
law of Christ. (Galatians 6:2)

God is love for *all*.

We are to be humble and kind. We are to be like Christ,
who treated everyone the same. Christ loved and went out of
his way to help others with their burdens.

We should do likewise.

SEPTEMBER 18

My voice shalt thou hear in the morning, O LORD:
In the morning will I direct my prayer unto thee,
and will look up. (Psalm 5:3)

Start every morning with prayer.

The most important thing you can do every morning is pray. Don't get out of bed until you pray, saying, "Thank you, Lord!"

Don't walk out the door before you pray. Pray for protection and guidance for you and your family.

Pray. Just do it! Watch God work in your life and your family.

SEPTEMBER 19

> Casting *all* your care upon him for he careth for you. (1 Peter 5:7, emphasis added)

Yes, God cares for *you*—always!

Be confident that he is with you—every day, every second, in all situations.

SEPTEMBER 19

For all have sinned, and come short of the glory of God. (Romans 3:23)

The verse tells us "all have sinned"—that is you and me. Thank you, Jesus, for taking away our sins!

SEPTEMBER 20

For the wages of sin is death; but the gift of God is eternal life through Jesus Christ our Lord. (Romans 6:23)

There is no greater gift than eternal life. Thank you, Jesus! I'll see you when God brings my soul home.

Will *you* see Jesus?

SEPTEMBER 21

Humble yourselves therefore under the mighty
hand of God, that he may *exalt* you in due time.
(1 Peter 5:6, emphasis added)

The word *exalt* means to praise or worship; to make higher in
rank, power, or dignity; to fill with happiness and pride.

God wants to exalt you. The time is coming when you will
be with him.

Do you trust God? Do you believe Jesus died for you?

SEPTEMBER 22

But God commanded his love toward us, in that, while we were yet sinners, Christ died for us. (Romans 5:8)

Thank you, God, for your love.
Thank you, Jesus, for dying for us.

SEPTEMBER 23

But I have trusted in thy mercy; my heart shall rejoice in thy salvation. (Psalm 13:5)

Trust God.

Our hearts know God's love, and our souls rejoice with God's gift of salvation. Thank you, Lord.

Rejoice, knowing that when you die with Jesus, your soul will be in heaven. What a blessing of assurance and peace.

SEPTEMBER 24

Neither is there salvation in any other; for there
is none other name under heaven given among
men, whereby we must be saved. (Acts 4:12)

The one and only Jesus is the way to be saved. He is your only
way to salvation. Not your way but Christ's way!

Choose Jesus. Choose heaven. Choose to spend eternity in
heaven!

SEPTEMBER 25

Let this mind be in you, which was also in Christ
Jesus. (Philippians 2:5)

May my mind and my heart be like Jesus's mind and heart.
May your mind and your heart be like Jesus's mind and heart.
Thank you, Jesus, for your love and example for us.

SEPTEMBER 26

I will both lay me down in peace and sleep:
for thou, LORD, only makest me dwell in safety.
(Psalm 4:8)

Everyone has experienced going to bed when worried and concerned. Sleep seems impossible. Psalm 4:8 is a reminder to take everything to our Lord.

Give him your worries and problems, and he will give you peace and safety. Just give it all to God and let go.

Thank you, Lord!

SEPTEMBER 27

For God hath *not* given us the spirit of fear: but of power, and of love, and of a sound mind. (2 Timothy 1:7, emphasis added)

Thank you, God, for being with me to face every situation. You are the Almighty and have power over everything.

SEPTEMBER 28

The LORD is my strength and song, and he is become my salvation: he is my God, and I will prepare him as habitation; my father's God, and I will exalt him. (Exodus 15:2)

God gives you daily blessings!

Thou wilt keep him in perfect peace, whose mind is *stayed* on thee; because he trusteth in thee. (Isaiah 26:3, emphasis added)

Perfect peace can be found *only* in God. Keep your mind and heart on searching for and feeling God's peace and his plans for you.

Trust in God daily in all you do!

SEPTEMBER 29

Trust ye in the LORD forever: for in the LORD
JEHOVAH is everlasting strength. (Isaiah 26:4)

Everything comes from trusting the Lord, which comes only
from totally giving your heart to God and having the Holy Spirit
inside you.

You will have everlasting strength with the Holy Spirit.

Trust ye in the Lord!

SEPTEMBER 30

But thou, O LORD art a shield for me; my glory,
and the lifter up of mine head. (Psalm 3:3)

When I've been down and out, God—*only* God—brought me
up. Thank you, Lord!

OCTOBER 1

The L ORD is my light and my salvation; whom
shall I fear? The L ORD is the strength of my life;
of whom shall be afraid? (Psalm 27:1)

I think of David and his confidence when he faced Goliath.
   God, give me that strength and confidence.
   With God, I will not be afraid!

OCTOBER 2

And he [Jesus] saith unto them, "Why are ye fearful, O ye of little faith?" Then he arose, and rebuked the winds and the sea: and there was a great calm. (Matthew 6:26)

My Jesus is powerful. He controls the winds and seas; he can take care of me and my family.

OCTOBER 3

Be thou exalted Lord, in thine own strength: so will we sing and praise thy power. (Psalm 21:13)

The Lord brings joy to my soul.
He gives us all the strength we need.

OCTOBER 4

Nor height, not depth; nor any other creature, shall be able to separate us, from the love of God, which is Christ Jesus our Lord. (Romans 8:39)

God's love is final. He will not leave us, and nothing can separate us from God.

OCTOBER 5

He giveth power to the faint; and to them that
have no might, he increaseth strength. (Isaiah
40:29)

I have heard many stories from survivors of war and battles.
They say they felt God with them, and they kept going, even
when they thought they couldn't go anymore. The same is true
of sickness, whether mental or physical pain. God is with you!
Feel his power and strength!

OCTOBER 6

I love the LORD, because he hath heard my voice and my supplications.
Because he inclined his ear unto me, therefore will I call upon him as long as I live. (Psalm 116:1–2)

God has been with me every second of my life and continues to be with me. He has provided a lifetime of help, comfort, peace, and healing.

He is with you too.

I will continue all the days of my life to trust God.

I pray that you do the same.

OCTOBER 7

Shew me thy ways, O Lord; teach me thy paths.
Lead me in thy truth, and teach me: for thou art
the God of my salvation; on thee do I wait all the
day. (Psalm 25:4–5)

Lord, teach us that if we will open our eyes, ears, and heart, we
will feel your presence in everything we do.

God *will* open up your understanding when you are willing.

OCTOBER 8

And let the peace of God rule in your hearts to
the which also ye are called in one body; and be
ye thankful. (Colossians 3:15)

It's feels so good to be at peace. It's a time when you feel no
stress, no fear, and no anxiety, and you feel a calm you can't
explain. Only God can give you true peace.

Thank you, God, for peace for my mind, body, and soul.

OCTOBER 9

I will bless the L\ord at *all* times his praise
shall continually be in my mouth. (Psalm 34:1,
emphasis added)

Show and tell what the Lord is to you and what he has done for
you. Be a witness for God daily to anyone and everyone.

OCTOBER 10

For which cause we faint not; but though our outward man perish, yet the inward man is renewed day by day. (2 Corinthians 4:16)

We all get weary, tired, worn out, and exhausted with our earthly bodies, but our souls don't weary if God lives within us.

If God lives within us and we have accepted Jesus as our Savior, our souls will never age. We will have a renewed soul each day as we prepare for heaven.

My body and my outward circumstances and things around me will perish, but my inward spirit is renewed because of God.

OCTOBER 11

For I will pour water upon him that is thirsty, and floods upon the dry ground: I will pour my spirit upon thy seed, and my blessing upon thine off-spring. (Isaiah 44:3)

God provides for our needs!

Thank you, Lord, for promising to give blessings to my family in all generations.

OCTOBER 12

He keepth the paths of judgement, and preserveth the way of his saints. (Proverbs 2:8)

Thank you, Lord, for being a just God.
God expects the best in you.

OCTOBER 13

Let everything that hath breath praise the LORD.
Praise ye the LORD. (Psalm 150:6)

Every day and in everything, give God the praise.
Every day.
In everything.

OCTOBER 14

By him therefore let us offer the sacrifice of praise to God continually, that is, the fruit of our lips giving thanks to this name. (Hebrews 13:15)

Praise God—always and continually.

Give thanks to him. Say, "Thank you, God," every morning, noon, and night!

OCTOBER 15

Thus saith the LORD, which maketh a way in the sea, and a path in the mighty waters. (Isaiah 43:16)

God can and will make a way just for you.
    In God we trust!

OCTOBER 16

And they shall be my people, and I will be their God. And I will give them one heart, and one way, that they may fear me for ever, for the good of them, and of their children after them. (Jeremiah 32:38–39)

Serve God and fear him forever.
He is the almighty power.

OCTOBER 17

For the LORD is good; his mercy is everlasting:
and his truth endureth to all generations. (Psalm
100:5)

In God we trust. We trust his goodness, truth, and everlasting
mercy.

OCTOBER 18

Behold, the LORD, GOD will come with a strong hand, and his arm shall rule for him, behold, his reward is with him, and his work before him. (Isaiah 40:10)

God is the Almighty, his power and reward. What a promise, just for you.

OCTOBER 19

Now faith is the substance of things hoped for,
the evidence of things not seen. (Hebrews 11:1)

Have faith in God. Trust in God. Faith and trust go together.
God is with you!

OCTOBER 20

Now therefore thus saith the LORD of hosts: consider *your* ways. ... Thus saith the LORD of hosts; consider *your* ways. (Haggai 1:5, 7, emphasis added)

Do you want God to bless your home and your family? Consider your ways.

OCTOBER 21

For the Kingdom of God is not meat and drink; but righteousness, and peace, and joy in the Holy Ghost. (Romans 14:17)

God promises righteousness and peace.
True joy comes only from the Holy Ghost.
Thank you, Jesus, for the kingdom of God.

OCTOBER 22

Nevertheless *we, according* to his *promise*, look for new heavens and a new earth, where is dwelleth righteousness. (2 Peter 3:13, emphasis added)

I'm looking forward to all God's promises.
Are you ready? Are you looking forward to it all?

OCTOBER 23

In my distress I cried unto the LORD, and he heard me. (Psalm 120:1)

Everyone has been distressed at some point in their lives.

When we turn to God, he hears us and comforts us, and he gives peace.

Keep praying during your distress and the distress of others. God is there, and he is listening.

OCTOBER 24

In the beginning God created the heaven and the earth. (Genesis 1:1)

Thank you, God. How powerful and wonderful is your might!
Do you think he can help you in any situation? Do you think there is anything he can't do? He is the Almighty, the maker of everything—and that includes you.

OCTOBER 25

But is from thence thou shalt seek the LORD thy God, thou shalt find him, if thou seek him with *all thy heart* and with *all thy soul*. (Deuteronomy 4:29, emphasis added)

Seek God!
　　Always seek God!
　　He *is* there!

OCTOBER 26

Jesus said:

> I am the true vine, and my Father is the
> husbandman. (John 12:1)

The word *husbandman* means a person who cultivates the land.
Jesus is the real truth that God cultivates.

Are you a vine off the true vine? Are you growing and
thriving? Are you growing daily?

OCTOBER 27

Let all the earth fear the Lord: let all the inhabitants of the world stand in awe of him.
(Psalm 33:8)

Open your heart, your eyes, and your ears. God is powerful over the whole world!

OCTOBER 28

I wait for the Lord, my Soul doth wait, and in his word do I hope. (Psalm 130:5)

From birth to death, we wait on the Lord's timing to bring our souls back to him.

We *can't keep* the old life and have a new life.

OCTOBER 29

For the eyes of the Lord are over the righteous, and his ears are open unto their prayers: but the face of the Lord is against them that do evil. (1 Peter 3:12)

Thank you, Lord, for listening to our prayers and helping us against evil. Help us daily to see evil and to fight it!

OCTOBER 30

Go to the ant, thou sluggard: consider *her* ways,
and be wise. (Proverbs 6:6, emphasis added)

Don't quit—that means, don't be a sluggard; don't be lazy.
Keep busy, and be wise.

OCTOBER 31

But now, O Lord, thou art our father; we are the clay, and thou our potter; and we *all* are the work of thy hand. (Isaiah 64:8, emphasis added)

I delight to do they will, O my God: yea, thy law is within my heart. (Psalm 40:8)

God made us all! We should live like the children of the Almighty God.

Thank you, God, for our daily blessings.

NOVEMBER 1

The LORD is good, a strong hold in the day of trouble; and he knoweth them that trust in him. (Nahum 1:7)

My God is strong! In him I trust—everything!
Go face the world and all of its problems. God is with you.

NOVEMBER 2

Jesus said:

> Blessed are the poor in spirit; for theirs is the
> kingdom of heaven. (Matthew 5:3)

Your spirit is blessed. Are you a blessing to others? Share
Jesus's love with others who need you.

NOVEMBER 3

Blessed are they that mourn, for they shall be comforted. (Matthew 5:4)

Thank you, Lord, for the blessings of the ones I mourn. You sent the right people into my life at the right time. I realize only you can give comfort to me and others.

I pray that others will feel your comfort as I do.

NOVEMBER 4

Blessed are the meek: for they shall inherit the
earth. (Matthew 5:5)

The word *meek* refers to being quiet, gentle, patient, and
long-suffering.

Are you meek?

Most of the time, I need to work on that. I want to be meek,
so I'll keep working. I hope that you are already meek. God
expects us to be meek.

NOVEMBER 5

Blessed are they which do hunger and thirst after righteousness; for they shall be filled. (Matthew 5:6)

We all want righteousness and goodness. Jesus promises to fill us and bless us if we turn to him.

Have you turned to Jesus to feed your soul? Do you long to have Jesus as your Savior? He's there for you.

NOVEMBER 6

Blessed are the merciful; for they shall obtain
mercy. (Matthew 5:7)

The word *mercy* means compassion or forgiveness. If you want
God to forgive you, you must forgive others. Then you will be
blessed.

NOVEMBER 7

Blessed are the pure in heart: for they shall see God. (Matthew 5:8)

Is your heart pure? If not, fix it!
We all want to see God.

NOVEMBER 8

Blessed are the peacemakers: for they shall be
called the children of God. (Matthew 5:9)

Peacemaker refers to a person who brings about peace. Is
that you?

Do you want to be called a child of God? If so, accept Jesus
as God's Son and your Savior. What a wonderful feeling of love,
comfort, and peace when *you know* you are a child of God!

NOVEMBER 9

Blessed are they which are persecuted for
righteousness' sake: for theirs is the Kingdom
of heaven. (Matthew 5:10)

Stand for God. Live life with Jesus. It is hard to go against evil
and stand up for what is right in God's eyes and laws.

Satan has evil working harder than ever.

Be strong, like the many people in the Bible who were
persecuted for God. We serve and worship the same God today.

NOVEMBER 10

Exalt the Lord our God, and worship at his holy
hill: for the Lord our God is holy. (Psalm 99:9)

The word *exalt* means to hold someone or something in very
high regard; to think or speak very highly.

Do you *exalt* God? It's time to do so. Exalt God today and
every day. You will see how good it feels and the blessings you
will receive.

NOVEMBER 11

Behold, I will bring it health and cure, and I will cure them, and will reveal unto them the abundance of peace and truth. (Jeremiah 33:6)

Thank you, Lord, for your promises.

Thank you for your abundance of peace and truth that can come *only* from you!

NOVEMBER 12

As I live, saith the LORD GOD, surely with a mighty hand, and with a stretched out arm, and with fury poured out, will I rule over you. (Ezekiel 20:33)

My God is *mighty*!
I want to pray for his blessings, not his fury.

NOVEMBER 13

And the Kingdom and dominion and the *greatness* of the kingdom under the *Whole heaven*, shall be given to the people of the saints of the most High, whose Kingdom is an *everlasting Kingdom,* and all dominions shall *Serve* and *obey him*. (Daniel 7:27, emphasis added)

We must serve and obey. Heaven expects it!

NOVEMBER 14

The Lord is nigh unto them that are of a broken
heart: and saveth such as be of a contrite spirit.
(Psalm 34:18)

The word *contrite* means to feel or express remorse or penitence;
affected by guilt.

God is with you when your heart is broken. He is with the
contrite (sincere) spirit.

Be sincere with God. *He is with you!*

NOVEMBER 15

I delight to do thy will, O my God: yea, thy law is within my heart. (Psalm 40:8)

It feels good to do God's will and obey him.
Try it today.

NOVEMBER 16

Teach me good judgement and knowledge: for I have believed thy commandments. (Psalm 119:66)

Ask and believe—God made it simple. You don't need another translation of the Bible.

Have you read the Ten Commandments lately? Read Exodus 20 to refresh your memory.

NOVEMBER 17

Even a child is known by his doing, whether his work be pure, and whether it be right. (Proverbs 20:11)

As children, we all learn right from wrong and good from evil.

Nothing changes when we become adults—right or wrong, good or evil.

God or Satan—you choose!

NOVEMBER 18

And the Lord shall guide thee continually, and satisfy they soul in drought, and make fat they bones: and thou shalt be like a watered garden, and like a spring of water, whose waters fail not.
(Isaiah 58:11)

The Lord is continual. He's not a part-time or a hit-or-miss God. He is there to satisfy your soul.

NOVEMBER 19

For I *am* the *am*: I will speak and the word that I shall speak shall come to pass; it shall be no more prolonged: for in your days, O rebellious house, will I say to word, and will perform it, saith the Lord God. (Ezekiel 12:25, emphasis added)

It will be exactly as God said—*exactly*.

His Word does not change for human beings or their feelings or emotions.

NOVEMBER 20

Daniel answered and said, Blessed be the name of God for ever and ever: for wisdom and might are his. (Daniel 2:20)

Thank you, Lord, for your wisdom and might.
I want to have faith like Daniel's.

NOVEMBER 21

Therefore turn thou to they God: Keep mercy
and judgement and wait on thy God continually.
(Hosea 12:6)

Always, *always* turn to God. Continually keep with God's
promises.

NOVEMBER 22

Therefore also now, saith the LORD, turn ye even
to me with all your heart, and with fasting, and
with weeping, and with mourning. (Joel 2:12)

Everyone will die.

Everyone has to cope with the loss when loved ones die.

Everyone will cry and mourn during his or her lifetime.

Turn to God with your soul and heart for comfort and peace.

NOVEMBER 23

And I prayed unto the LORD my God, and made my confession, and said, O LORD, the great and dreadful God, Keeping the covement and mercy to them that love him, and to them that keep his commandments. (Daniel 9:4)

Pray. Love God. Keep God's commandments.
    It's not hard; just *do* it!

NOVEMBER 24

Therefore say thou unto them, Thus saith the LORD of hosts; Turn ye unto me, saith the LORD of hosts; and I will turn unto you, saith the LORD of hosts. (Zechariah 1:3)

Turn to our Lord. He's waiting for you.

NOVEMBER 25

And I will strengthen them in the Lord; and they
shall walk up and down in this name, saith the
Lord. (Zechariah 10:12)

Thank you, Lord, for giving me strength when I am weak and
tired.

My sweet sister died on this date, two days before her
seventh birthday. I don't understand, but I trust God.

There *will* be a day of rejoicing again. Thank you, Lord.

NOVEMBER 26

And *Jesus saith* unto him, "The foxes have holes, and the birds of the air have nests; but the Son of man hath not where to lay his head. (Matthew 8:20, emphasis added)

Jesus is with us, everywhere, every time!
He *cares.*

NOVEMBER 27

But Jesus said, Suffer little children and forbid them not, to come unto me: for of such is the kingdom of heaven. (Matthew 19:14)

And [Jesus said,] The time is fulfilled, and the Kingdom of God is at hand: repent ye, and believe the gospel. (Mark 1:15)

There is *no* time to wait or to put off believing in Jesus. He said, "The kingdom of God is at hand."
Repent *now.* Believe the Bible!

NOVEMBER 28

For I know the thoughts that I think toward you, saith the LORD, thoughts of peace, and not of evil, to give you and expected end. (Jeremiah 29:11)

God has plans just for you. God wants the best for you!

God loves to see you succeed and to be a witness for the blessings he has given you. Be blessed.

In God we trust—everything and every day.

NOVEMBER 29

Jesus said:

> And thou shalt love the Lᴏʀᴅ they God with all
> they heart, and with all thy soul, and with all
> they mind, and with all thy strength; this is the
> first commandment. (Mark 12:30)

Jesus said that you must use your heart, soul, mind, and strength for God. Do you?

NOVEMBER 30

My soul melteth for heaviness: strengthen thou
me according unto they word. (Psalm 119:28)

When your soul is tired, weary, and heavy, ask God to give you
strength. This he has promised!

DECEMBER 1

My flesh and my heart faileth: but God is the
strength of my heart, and my portion forever.
(Psalm 73:26)

God has picked me up when I couldn't go on. When everything
was hopeless, he brought back my strength in my soul and my
heart.

In God we trust—over and over.

DECEMBER 2

I will love thee, O Lord, my strength. The Lord is my rock, and my fortress, and my deliverer: my God, my strength, in whom I will trust: my buckler, and the horn of my salvation, and my high tower. (Psalm 18:1–2)

God takes care of it *all.* Believe. Trust. Pray.

DECEMBER 3

Jesus said:

> These things I have spoken unto you, that in me ye might have peace, in the world ye shall have tribulation: but be of good cheer: I have overcome the world. (John 16:33)

Jesus overcame the world. He is there for you.
We all have trials, heartaches, and many tribulations, but Jesus is with us.

DECEMBER 4

Be strong and of a good courage, fear not, nor
be afraid of them: for the LORD the God, he it is
that doth go with thee; he will not fail thee, nor
forsake thee. (Deuteronomy 31:6)

You are *not* alone!
God does not fail you.
Trust and pray!

DECEMBER 5

The LORD shall fight for you, and ye shall hold
your peace. (Exodus 14:14)

Do you feel that you don't have any fight left in you? Give all
your problems to God. You will find peace when God takes your
problems.

DECEMBER 6

For the LORD your God is he that goeth with you,
to fight for you against your enemies, to save
you. (Deuteronomy 20:4)

Thank you, Lord!

I am never alone because you are with me. In God I trust
during tough, fearful times.

DECEMBER 7

And our hope of you is stedfast, Knowing, that
as ye are partakers of suffering, so shall ye be
also of the consolation. (2 Corinthians 1:7)

God is dependable and steadfast in everything. He is with us in
all our suffering.
He will give peace and comfort.

DECEMBER 8

Grace to you, and peace from God our Father
and the Lord Jesus Christ. (Philemon 1:3)

You! It's all for you—grace and peace—and it's from God our
Father and Lord Jesus Christ.

Feel the comfort of knowing that you are special. God
loves *you*.

DECEMBER 9

I thank my God, making mention of thee always
in my prayers. (Philemon 1:4)

Do you thank God for the people in your life? Do you always pray?

Be thankful and pray for family, friends, coworkers, your church, your pastor—everyone can use prayer.

God listens!

DECEMBER 10

Let us hold fast the profession of our faith without wavering; (for he is faithful that promised;) (Hebrews 10:23)

Don't let your faith waver. God is faithful, and his promises make your faith stronger.

In God we trust!

DECEMBER 11

But the word of the Lord endureth for ever. And this is the word which by the gospel is preached unto you. (1 Peter 1:25)

My grandparents and probably your grandparents owned and read the King James Bible. Many learned to read with a Bible; it sometimes was the only book in the house.

"The word of the Lord endureth forever."

Thank you, Lord, for the Bible. I can't imagine life without the Bible. I treasure it; I hope you do too.

DECEMBER 12

For even here unto were ye called: because
Christ also suffered for us leaving us an example,
that ye should follow his steps. (1 Peter 2:21)

Christ suffered and died for us—for you and me.

He left us a perfect example of the lives we should live. We
need to follow his steps!

DECEMBER 13

For thus saith the LORD God, the Holy One of Israel: In returning and rest shall ye be saved; In quietness and in confidence shall be your strength: and ye would not. (Isaiah 30:15)

God's with you—always. He will give you rest, quietness, confidence, and strength.

"Thus saith [says] the Lord God."

DECEMBER 14

According to the eternal purpose which he
purposed in Christ Jesus our Lord: In whom we
have boldness and access with confidence by
the faith of him. (Ephesians 3:11–12)

What are your eternal plans? You will die, but where will your
soul spend eternity?

Choose and serve Christ Jesus, our Lord. He promises
boldness and access to him with confidence at all times. Have
faith.

Thank you, Jesus!

DECEMBER 15

I will praise thee, for I am fearfully and
wonderfully made: marvelous are thy works:
and that my soul knoweth right well. (Psalm
139:14)

Give God all praise each day. He will provide just for you. He
knows your soul and what is best for you.

In God we trust.

DECEMBER 16

The wicked shall be turned into hell, and all the
nations that forget God. (Psalm 9:17)

There *is* a heaven and a hell. Do you choose Jesus and heaven,
or do you choose Satan and hell?

Please don't forget God. Live for *him*! Pray and seek God
daily.

DECEMBER 17

O, Lᴏʀᴅ our Lᴏʀᴅ how excellent is the name in all the earth! Who hast set they glory above the heavens. (Psalm 8:1)

Our Lord is known worldwide, all over the earth. His glory shines from heaven.

Are you ready to meet him in heaven?

DECEMBER 18

Jesus said:

> Whosoever therefore shall confess me before
> men, him will I confess also before my Father,
> which is in heaven. (Matthew 10:32)

Are you known as a Christian? Do you confess Jesus as your Savior? Do you live as God wants you to live?

Jesus will be in heaven to introduce you.

DECEMBER 19

Jesus said:

> And then shall they see the Son of man coming
> in the clouds with great power and glory. (Mark
> 13:26)

Look up at the clouds. Imagine that Jesus is coming for you and your family and friends.

Can you smile with the thought of the amazing, powerful shining glory? If not, accept Jesus as your Savior and share that with family and friends.

DECEMBER 20

Jesus said:

> No man, when he hath lighted a candle, putteth
> it in a secret place, neither under a bushel, but
> on a candle stick, that they which come in may
> see the light. (Luke 11:33)

One of my favorite children's songs is "This Little Light of Mine":

> This little light of mine
> I'm gonna let it shine

God wants your Christian light to shine.

> Let it shine, all the time, let it shine.

DECEMBER 21

Jesus said:

> For every one that doeth evil hateth the light,
> neither cometh to the light, lest his deeds should
> be reproved But he that doeth truth cometh to
> the light that his deeds may be made manifest,
> that they are wrought in God. (John 3:20–21)

Jesus is the light, and he shines. People who believe go to the light.

Sinners and evildoers go away from the light and Jesus. They don't want the truth (the light) to show their sins.

In which direction do you go?

DECEMBER 22

Jesus said:

> For what is a man profited, if he shall gain the whole world, and lose his own soul? Or what shall a man give in exchange for his soul? (Matthew 16:26)

Do you work so that you can have all the worldly possessions and luxuries you want? Do you dream of being rich and successful? Is that your goal?

Stop! Will you stop focusing more on earthly goals? These will cost you your soul and your relationship with God.

Which possessions will gain you eternity?

DECEMBER 23

But now thus saith the Lord that created thee, O
Jacob, and the that formed thee, O Israel, Rear
not: for I have redeemed thee, I have called thee
by thy name; thou art mine. (Isaiah 43:1)

I love it when God says, "Fear not," and he knows you and me
personally, by name.

I know I can trust God.

DECEMBER 24

The Lord shall fight for you, and ye shall hold
your peace. (Exodus 14:14)

When God is *for* you, who would dare to challenge you?

God wants peace, trust, and eternity for you. Go out and
face your problems—with God!

DECEMBER 25

How precious also are thy thoughts unto me.
O God! how great is the sum of them. (Psalm
139:17)

Thank you, God, for thoughts of me.

God has plans for each of us. God loves you and wants only
the best for and from you.

Christmas shows God's love for you. He gave you the
greatest gift—his precious Son, Jesus. He gave you the gift of
eternal life—if you accept his holy Son, Jesus.

Share this gift of love with others on this day and for the
rest of your life.

DECEMBER 26

For I know the thoughts that I think toward you, saith the LORD, thoughts of peace, and not of evil, to give you an expected end. (Jeremiah 29:11)

No one knows my thoughts but God.

God, I want to have thoughts that please you. May my thoughts be of peace.

DECEMBER 27

He only is my rock and my salvation: he is my
defence; I shall not be moved. In God is my
salvation and my glory: the rock of my strength,
and my refuge, is in God. *Trust* in him at *all*
times; ye people, pour out your heart before
him: God is a refuge for us. Se'lah. (Psalm 62:6–
8, emphasis added)

Selah means "forever."
In God we trust. Say it every day.

DECEMBER 28

Teaching them to observe all things whatsoever
I have commanded you: and, lo, I am with you
always, even unto the end of the world. Amen.
(Matthew 28:20)

What a promise—that God will never leave us and will be with
us forever!

In God we trust—always, forever.

DECEMBER 29

Every word of God is pure; he is a shield unto them that put their trust in him. (Proverbs 30:5)

You are not alone, not ever!
God is *with* you. Put your trust in him.

DECEMBER 30

> Preserve me, O God: for in thee do I put my trust. (Psalm 16:1)

I trust God—and I wear my seatbelt.

I trust God—and I use oven mitts with hot dishes.

I trust God—and I lock my house.

I trust God—and I take my prescribed medicines.

I trust God with all things that I cannot control.

I trust God to be with me and protect me with all things unseen.

I trust God!

Do *you*?

DECEMBER 31

O, Keep my soul, and deliver me: let me not be ashamed; for I put my trust in thee. (Psalm 25:20)

Dear Lord,

Please help me to be thankful and to feel blessed for all things you have done and given me.

Dear Lord, please deliver my soul to heaven when you have completed your plan for me on earth.

Dear Lord, please give family, friends, students, neighbors, community, and our world the peace of eternal life with you, though Jesus, your Son.

I have trusted you in everything. You have answered prayer after prayer in many ways that I could not imagine.

Thank you, Lord!

In God we (I) trust!

CPSIA information can be obtained
at www.ICGtesting.com
Printed in the USA
JSHW030024300123
36842JS00007B/8